There's no other city in A[...]
and grandiose than New Y[...]
that allows groundbreakin[...]
Nothing seems to faze New Yorkers: not the tight quarters,
not the noise pollution, not even the G train... it seems Gothamists
are intrinsically capable of facing any provocation or adversity.
So what exactly is the trade off? The aspiring singer on the
subway who had everyone smiling during their commute,
those 4am pastrami excursions and the bewitching air of being
surrounded by over eight million innovative residents.

It's a city that encourages you to seek out and listen to the many
multi-ethnic and multi-generational stories full of creativity,
grit and passion that are told with great pride (justifiably so,
because they worked hard for it, dammit). From family-owned
businesses to artist studios funded by Kickstarter campaigns,
there are so many places to visit that you may develop a serious
case of FOMO. Though it might take a lifetime to check mark
everything on your NYC to-do list, this guide is a primer for how
to spend your New York minute.

## the hunt new york city writer

### joanna kang

JoAnna admits it took her years to make the cross country move from
Portland, Oregon to New York City. She finally confronted NYC's cramped,
well-oiled machine, churning out long workdays in exchange for living in a
24-hour glutton's paradise. Ignoring the fact that her armoire is four feet from
the stove, she enjoys recreating delicious recipes from Elizabeth David cookbooks
and being part of the team at Windfall Farms's stand at the Union Square
Greenmarket, which advocates pesticide-free, non-GMO, unconventionally
grown produce.

# where to lay your weary head

*Rest up, relax and recharge*

# DISTRIKT HOTEL

*Utilitarian stay*

342 West 40th Street (near 9th Avenue; Midtown West) / +1 212 706 6100
distrikthotel.com

Double from $161

Distrikt Hotel is for the savvy traveler whose itinerary is typed out to the minute, hoping to catch every attraction in town. Located between Port Authority and Times Square, every major train line is in close proximity so guests can commute with ease. With New York City-themed décor, including a 12-foot living wall in the lobby representing Central Park, and high-class hospitality and facilities, Distrikt Hotel will rest weary heads and tired tourist feet in style.

# LAFAYETTE HOUSE

*Pre-war brownstone*

38 East 4th Street (near Cooper Square; East Village)
+1 212 505 8100 / lafayettehousenyc.com

Double from $300

Formerly a pre-war apartment complex, Lafayette House has 15 cozy bedrooms. Each one has a functioning marble fireplace, and some even have a kitchenette and private patio, so if you'd like to pretend you're in your very own pad, snag one of those. I overhear a lot of tourists say, "I love visiting NYC, but I'd never want to live here." Well, after a night availing of Lafayette's charms, guests just might find themselves curiously scrolling through real estate listings over their morning coffee.

# MCCARREN HOTEL & POOL

*Contemporary luxury in an urban retreat*

160 North 12th Street (near Bedford Avenue; Williamsburg)
+1 718 218 7500 / mccarrenhotel.com

Double from $242

Water babies will find it difficult to resist the three-season, salt-water outdoor swimming pool here, one of the largest in NYC. As at the sister hotel in the heart of the city, McCarren Hotel & Pool offers luxurious hospitality and stylish furnishings in the form of bamboo floors, neutral beige and orange accents, and marble bathrooms.

# THE INN AT IRVING PLACE

*Historic hospitality*

54 Irving Place (near 17th Street; Gramercy) / +1 212 533 4600
innatirving.com

Double from $445

Built in 1834, this terraced-house hotel is a refuge from the city.
Minus possessing the coveted key for the private, fenced Gramercy Park
located merely a block away, guests will feel right at home in this clandestine,
sans-sign, Victorian-style townhouse. A refined interior including 12 guest
rooms and the elegant Lady Mendl's Tea Salon, this is a perfect place for a
quiet getaway. Pinkies up.

THE NOMAD HOTEL

# THE MARLTON HOTEL

*Beat Generation abode*

5 West 8th Street (near 5th Avenue; West Village) / +1 212 321 0100
marltonhotel.com

Double from $215

How apropos for a neighborhood known for its excruciatingly adorable
cafés to now have a charming Parisian-ascribed boutique hotel – that
also happens to serve raw almond cappuccinos at its espresso bar.
Well, I don't know how Parisian that last part sounded, but The Marlton
does deserve full credit for its romantic décor of marble floors, charming
molding and literary history. Over a century old, it has housed the likes of
John Barrymore, Jack Kerouac and Lenny Bruce. Rooms are small,
but comfortably stylish – ideal for discerning artists.

THE MARLTON

## THE NOMAD HOTEL

*Chic comfort with a top-notch restaurant*

1170 Broadway (near West 28th Street; NoMad) / +1 212 796 1500
thenomadhotel.com

Double from $375

Who can resist The NoMad's cocktail bar or the chance to snuggle with a
book in their library? Or enjoying the luxurious roast chicken stuffed
with foie gras in their constantly buzzing and overbooked restaurant?
Or dropping by for its weekly live magic show held on the second floor?
Lucky guests, because they can do all this knowing that once all the fun's
been had, bed is but an elevator ride away. The rooms have a classic,
timeless style inspired by the Parisian apartment home of the
designer's youth.

## WYTHE HOTEL

*Boutique chic*

80 Wythe Avenue (at North 11th Street; Williamsburg) / + 1 718 460 8000
wythehotel.com

Double from $235

The Ides, the Wythe Hotel's rooftop bar, arguably has one of the best
skyline views of Manhattan, where the jagged rows of colossal, concrete
stalagmites rise from the single narrow peninsula. The hotel's designer
wallpaper (from Flavor Paper) casually cushions the gritty, industrial
use of exposed brick and planks of dark wood, and the beds are made of
pine reclaimed from the building – a blend of grunge brought to you by a
collaboration of the best local artists, designers and architects.

# east village and lower east side

## financial district, tribeca

As of late, a barrage of strollers and young professionals enjoys TriBeCa's quaint, cobblestone streets, beautiful waterfront views and industrial sunlit lofts. Straight-shave barbers and shoe shiners still remain open for Wall Street worker bees in the Financial District, while in the East Village and the Lower East Side (LES.) – once home to vagabonds, drug dealers and defunct fabric stores – NYU dormitories and burgeoning independent art galleries abound. Here was the birthplace of artistic movements, punk rock and protests,and it remains a center of counterculture despite gentrification.

1  Chambers Street Wines (off map)
2  Fabulous Fanny's
3  Gohan (off map)
4  Korin (off map)
5  Maiden Lane
6  Maryam Nassir Zadeh
7  Pilgrim New York
8  Russ & Daughters
9  Spicy Village
10 Still House
11 Top Hat
12 Top Hops Beer Shop

# CHAMBERS STREET WINES

*Unparalleled biodynamic and organic wine selection*

**148 Chambers Street (near West Broadway)** / **+1 212 227 1434**
chambersstwines.com / **Open daily**

Oftentimes, stepping into a wine store can be as daunting as attempting to adapt to a foreign country, learning the language and understanding the culture. I've certainly encountered a few vino experts who rattle off Robert Parker quotes, their faces turning the color of grapes when I can't recall the number of hectares in Château-Chalon. Happily at Chambers Street Wines, such snobbery does not exist. The staff is passionate in educating and challenging drinkers to step out of their usual DOC and try something new. Head over to the 15-foot-long shelf of niche Champagne labels and start your journey of discovery.

# FABULOUS FANNY'S

*Eccentric wonderland for the visually impaired*

**335 East 9th Street (near 1st Avenue)** / **+1 212 533 0637**
**facebook.com/page/FabulousFannys** / **Open daily**

In second grade I became a secret squinter. Though sitting right in front of the chalkboard inadvertently typecast me as an overachiever, it wasn't until my mother caught on that I was forced to wear thick, red-rimmed, bifocal glasses that created years of provocation. Stepping into Fabulous Fanny's was like post-traumatic glasses-wearing therapy. The staff offers honest opinions to help you choose the right frames, the stock of which ranges from vintage 18th-century to modern designs. The selection is so massive, you'll wish you really had four-eyes to go through it all. Time to trade in my bifocals for vintage Emmanuelle Khanh and forever rid myself of torturous elementary school memories.

# GOHAN

*Sustainability-minded Japanese brick and mortar*

**14A Orchard Street (near Canal Street)** / **+1 646 590 1311**
**gohannyc.com** / **Open daily**

Regulars rejoiced when chef Atsushi Numata and his wife, Saori, expanded their successful Essex Street Market (see pg 84) stand to the more extensive Gohan. With their no-waste mentality, Atsushi and Saori go beyond gluten-free, vegan cooking, and focus on respecting the environment and supporting local ingredients: fresh fish come from Long Island daily and veggies are always sourced from the city's greenmarkets. Though health-minded restaurants pop up like wild chrysanthemum these days, Gohan isn't what you're picturing. Instead, 1970s Japanese punk blares within the playful setting filled with Heywood Wakefield school chairs and counters made from refurbished wood from old Kyoto farmhouses. Plus, inventive cuisine is served up and biodynamic, sparkling sake is poured.

# KORIN

*Japanese forged knives*

**57 Warren Street (near West Broadway) / +1 212 587 7021**
**korin.com / Open daily**

My craving for anything grilled increases exponentially with
awareness that barbecuing on an NY tenement rooftop is subject
to eviction. Growing up, my father, the grill master, lectured me on
the grades of charcoal and the importance of a sharp butchering
knife. Korin happens to offer both, including three different types
of Japanese charcoal and a collection of Japan-forged knives that
follows the Sakai knife craftsmanship – famous for its samurai swords.
Custom sharpening is offered by Master Chiharu Sugai via a whetting
wheel: one of two in the world that he himself designed.

# MAIDEN LANE

*Cured and specialty canned seafood*

**162 Avenue B (near East 10th Street)** / **+1 646 755 8911**
**themaidenlane.com** / **Open daily**

The whitefish salad at Maiden Lane blows tuna between slices of bread outta the water. Well, obviously. It might also have to do with the co-owners, Nialls Fallon and Gareth Maccubbin, curing their own fish, as well as sourcing some from ACME Smoked Fish. Who knew imported sardines and cockles, both from beautifully labeled cans, could taste so grand. Oil-slicked fillets from Jose Gourmet in Portugal, sold exclusively in the U.S. at Maiden Lane, gracefully swim amongst crunchy crudités. Surrender to the nautical theme and savor the pinewood planks of delicate sliced lox, creamy whitefish and uninterrupted glasses of briny sherry. Chin-chin!

# MARYAM NASSIR ZADEH

*Contemporary women's clothing*

**123 Norfolk Street (near Rivington Street)** / **+1 212 673 6405**
**mnzstore.com** / **Open daily**

In this beautiful store, the rows of gossamer silks and hand-tailored wool suits are carefully arranged, as if the hangers were painstakingly hung at a futuristic exhibition in the textile wing of a museum. Designer and co-owner Maryam Nassir Zadeh's relationship with art and travel is what makes this boutique a true shopping destination. Stepping into what feels more like a stark, white art gallery allows shoppers to stop and admire an accessory, a blanket or a shift dress, as if it's a colorful Kandinsky painting.

# PILGRIM NEW YORK

*The ultimate in vintage*

**70 Orchard Street (near Grand Street) / +1 212 463 7720**
**pilgrimnyc.com / Closed Monday**

When expanding one's collection of prized possessions, whether it's an obscure LP or mint-condition Hermès scarf, there's always someone who has the know-how in acquiring desired recherché. Luckily co-owners Richard Ives and Brian Bennett are seasoned sleuths in procuring vintage Chanel and Commes des Garçons, and selecting pieces made by specific designers during their reign at major fashion houses. Whether it's models hoarding outfits for casting calls or famous stylists hunting down a killer dress for an editorial shoot, Pilgrim New York works to obtain one-of-a-kind, mint-condition duds straight from private sellers. There's no attitude or noses yanked up by the strings of sales commissions here. No, there's only clever fashion advice and storytelling of fashion lore that'll steer loyal patrons clear of any buyer's remorse.

# RUSS & DAUGHTERS

*Golden child of appetizing shops*

**179 East Houston Street (near Orchard Street)** / **+1 212 475 4880**
russanddaughters.com / **Open daily**

Founder Joel Russ began his entrepreneurial venture behind a pushcart, from which witty, friendly service and fish expertise became, 100 years later, a store that The Smithsonian Institute tributes as "a part of New York's cultural heritage". Russ & Daughters maintains family traditions and is a historical and culinary golden child among NYC's mouthwatering Jewish shops. There's a reason why the best always outlasts the rest. To watch the venerable staff hand-slice velvety, paper-thin, smoked salmon while sampling hand-whipped scallion cream cheese is worth every minute of waiting in a congested, all-day queue. The knife skills, the banter, a handful of Hopjes, and, of course, the fish are all impossible to resist. I gush, but there is simply no other place as magical as Russ & Daughters, if you ask me.

# SPICY VILLAGE

*Hole-in-the-wall, Henan flavor*

**68 Forsyth Street (near Hester Street)** / **+1 212 625 8299**
**spicyvillageny.com** / **Open daily**

The only way for me to describe my feelings about Spicy Village is through a love song: "My Spicy Village; Sweet comic Spicy Village; You make me smile with my heart. Your looks are laughable; Unphotographable; Yet you're my favorite plate of food. Is your décor less than Greek; Is your light a little weak? When I open the door to eat; Are you bright? But don't change a spice for me; (Plus, your price is right for me); I'll stay and eat noodles all day; Each day is Spicy Village day." My apologies to Sinatra, but there's no way his Valentine was as good as these hand-pulled Chinese noodles.

# STILL HOUSE

*Precious gifts for friends and home*

**117 East 7th Street (near Avenue A) / +1 212 539 0200**
**stillhousenyc.com / Open daily**

Still House evokes everything the name describes: tranquility, warmth and simplicity. Owner Urte Tylaite carefully curates stunning jewelry, home goods and creative gifts. The former is spectacular, and always affordably priced. Pieces range from thin gold rings delicately dotted with precious, tiny diamonds to geometrically bold earrings. And even returning customers who just try on the same thing during every visit (i.e., me), are welcomed by the gracious Urte who acts as if she's hosting an intimate reception, and who answers all questions eruditely and with a smile — a dying trait in today's commercial world.

# TOP HAT

*A haven of home décor and stationery*

245 Broome Street (near Ludlow Street) / +1 212 677 4240
tophatnyc.com / Open daily

I popped into Top Hat to find a small gift for a fellow stationery lover.
Little did I know, owner Nina Allen offers more than the average pencil
case. It's a place where delicate French lace is sold by the yard. Oh, and
colorful Italian Ellepi staplers and the largest MT masking tape assortment
I've ever seen. If clerical workers walked the runway, Top Hat would be there
to clad them with all things necessary — and make them look good, too.
From intricate laser-cut bookmarks to Maison Martin Margiela notebooks,
Top Hat carries alluring, minimalist designs from all over the world.

# TOP HOPS

*Converter of beer snobs*

94 Orchard Street (near Broome Street) / +1 212 254 4677
tophops.com / Open daily

This is the most egalitarian craft bar I've ever stepped into. It's a place where hipsters, foodies and craft beer geeks saddle up along the bar to marvel at the 20 rotating taps from around the world. It's also a place to laugh at the flabbergasted blind tasters when Budweiser emerges a favorite among elitists. More importantly, there's an amazing beer list, with 700 bottles and cans for your tasting pleasure. And if all that imbibing whets your palate, delicious local snacks make for a perfect accompaniment. What's better than supporting local businesses and small breweries? I'll say cheers to that.

# brewed buzz

*Raising the coffee bar*

Experiencing caffeine withdrawal can exponentially drain one's energy. Though you can grab a lukewarm, watery cup of joe at any bodega, you shouldn't – instead, hit up these specialty slingers.

Tucked in Greenwich Village is **Caffé Reggio** and their 1902 espresso machine; it created their first cappuccino and the antique is now proudly displayed. Come for a shot of rich espresso and stay for the history and calming ambiance.

Duck into **Hi-Collar** in the East Village and order the flavorful iced pour-over. The cortado at **Happy Bones** will pacify one's patience while in SoHo sample sale lines, but if shopping isn't on your agenda, reserve a time slot at **Meow Parlour**. It's a wonderful place to sip on a mug full of Counter Culture roast and plan out the rest of your day while a furry feline naps in your lap.

Located on the ground floor of an Art Deco skyscraper in FiDi, **Black Fox Coffee** is where co-owners Daniel Murphy and Gary Hardwick and coffee director Kris Wood feature micro-roasters like Heart Roasters from Portland; Small Batch from Melbourne; and Brooklyn's own Parlor. Uptown? Swing by NYC's own micro-roaster, **Lenox Coffee**, for a single-origin cold brew.

Midtown is where the coffee compass goes haywire, but don't fret because **Hole In The Wall Coffee NYC** serves up NOVO Coffee's green java, and **Bibble & Sip**, whose signature matcha jasmine latte is so tasty it'll twist the arm of a purist, are both located near the Theater District.

In Brooklyn, Michelin Star-winning pastry chef Ryan Butler owns **Butler**, so you'll want his version of dark chocolate Babka on top of your cappuccino order. Take the B62 bus a few stops north and you'll find **Propeller Coffee**, a precious joint with free Wi-Fi and a West Coast feel. It's a place where drip coffee tastes good, and life seems to unfold a little slower for good reason.

### BLACK FOX COFFEE
70 Pine Street (near Pearl Street; Financial District)
no phone, blackfoxcoffee.com, closed Sunday

### BIBBLE & SIP
253 West 51st Street (near 8th Avenue; Midtown West)
+1 646 649 5116, bibbleandsip.com, open daily

### BUTLER
95 South 5th Street (at Berry Street; Williamsburg)
+1 718 489 8785, butler-nyc.com, open daily

### CAFFÉ REGGIO
119 MacDougal Street (near West 3rd Street;
Greenwich Village), +1 212 475 9557, caffereggio.com
open daily

### HAPPY BONES
394 Broome Street (near Mulberry Street; SoHo)
+1 212 673 3754, happybonesnyc.com, open daily

### HI-COLLAR
214 East 10th Street (near 2nd Avenue; East Village)
+1 212 777 7018, hi-collar.com, open daily

### HOLE IN THE WALL COFFEE NYC
420 5th Avenue (near East 38th Street;
Midtown East), +1 646 682 9510, holeinthewallnyc.com
closed Saturday and Sunday

### LENOX COFFEE
60 West 129th Street (at Lenox Avenue; Harlem)
+1 646 833 7839, lenoxcoffee.com, open daily

### MEOW PARLOUR
46 Hester Street (near Ludlow Street;
Lower East Side), no phone, meowparlour.com
closed Wednesday

### PROPELLER COFFEE
984 Manhattan Avenue
(near Huron Street; Greenpoint), +1 347 689 4777
cargocollective.com/propellercoffee, open daily

# soho

## chinatown, little italy, nolita

In Chinatown, prepare to haggle over the price of everything from designer contact lenses to cigarettes – observe and learn from the grandmothers who queue for dried shrimp; or, if you want to step out of the fray and do some people watching, head to nearby Mott Street. Some may scoff and consider SoHo nothing but an overgrown, outdoor shopping mall and food court, yet this neighborhood remains a trendy area with majestic, cast iron structures. Whereas SoHo has expanded with major, international stores, Nolita, a neighborhood east of Bowery, is where you'll find local designers and small, independent shops, along Elizabeth and Mulberry Streets. Further east, Little Italy is slowly seeing a demographic shift: Chinatown businesses have sprouted further down Mulberry and Mott Streets, and the demand for linguine with clams is gradually giving way to hand-pulled noodles and Hoisin sauce.

1 Anthom (off map)
2 Bánh Mì Saigon
3 Di Palo's Fine Foods
4 Estela
5 La Compagnie des Vins Surnaturale
6 Love Adorned
7 Michele Varian
8 Warm

# ANTHOM

*The ultimate creative clothing pilgrimage*

**25 Mercer Street (near Grand Street) / +1 877 747 1776**
**shopanthom.com / Open daily**

On the edge of SoHo, ANTHOM is a calming space of blond wood and neutral pastels where the inspiring story of a designer's vision is always told with candid enthusiasm. This storyteller is beyond any sales associate, and more like a docent in a minimalist art gallery sharing the philosophy of the "how it came to be" rather than the "why one must own it for thousands of dollars". Owner Ashley Turchin exemplifies an effortless refinement not defined by monetary status, and sales associates skitter across the runway-length room with clothes on copper hangers in tow. They share personal style advice with customers and take care to showcase high and low price points. For example, this shop carries everything from South Korean fashion darling Yune Ho's complete collection to up-and-coming designs by indie designer Ashley Rowe, whose fabrics are manipulated by hand from her trailer in Marfa, Texas.

# BÁNH MÌ SAIGON

*Vietnamese on the go*

**198 Grand Street (near Mott Street)** / **+1 212 941 1541**
banhmisaigonnyc.com / **Open daily**

In New York, skipping meals can quickly become the norm, especially when stuck in a hectic work-driven environment. Soon, a Snickers bar and coconut water from a bodega is considered a breakfast for champions. But a quick meal can also be one much more worth eating. Bánh Mì Saigon is a place where a five-dollar foot-long doesn't consist of corporate cold cuts. Rather, flavorful warm meats such as barbecued pork and curried chicken are enveloped inside fluffy French bread with a crackling crust. So, no more excuses with the sugar-crash caprice: make way for a bánh mì with a side order of thick, crunchy slabs of savory homemade shrimp chips.

# DI PALO'S FINE FOODS

*Italian specialty store*

**200 Grand Street (at Mott Street)** / **+1 212 226 1033**
dipaloselects.com / **Open daily**

We had friends over for an impromptu dinner, and they brought meat and cheese to go with our wine, salad and bread. I had one slice of the mortadella, then another, and suddenly I was eyeing it sideways, trying to calculate how I could eat the rest without anyone noticing. The very next day, I got myself to Di Palo's for more. When a grocer has been around for more than 100 years and still has a line out of the door all day, you know they're doing something right. At Di Palo's that something is everything Italian – ricotta made daily, imported prosciutto and parmesan, and the best mortadella and provolone sandwiches ever. Take a queue number and use the wait to decide: smoked mozzarella, burrata, or both?

# ESTELA

*Sharable plates of culinary wonder*

**47 East Houston Street (near Mulberry Street) / +1 212 219 7693**
**estelanyc.com / Open daily**

Growing up in the Northwest, I had the opportune chance of befriending foragers who once invited me on an expedition. With a death grip around my handheld GPS, the time spent in search for porcini mushrooms was a humbling experience – especially when returning home with only a handful of lowly grade no. 3's. The cuisine at Estela recalls such memories, as every pristine ingredient is like a hiding bolete or spectacular cilantro sauce waiting to be discovered. It's a beautiful environment where comfort meets precision. Chef Ignacio Mattos creates dishes meant for sharing, but after everyone's had their fair share you'll want to repeat the same order, reveling in the ephemeral flavors all by yourself.

# LA COMPAGNIE DES VINS SURNATURELS

*Wonderful wines*

**249 Centre Street (near Broome Street) / +1 212 343 3660**
**compagnienyc.com / Open daily**

Certain signs point to a great wine bar: the curated allocations,
the integrity of the wines by the glass, the atmosphere. Then there's
La Compagnie des Vins Surnaturels, which makes hospitality look like a
doorstop. Though their name implies carrying natural wine, with the play
on the word "supernatural," they not-so-subtly roast the idea of trendiness.
All agriculture politics aside, this bar à vin is an inviting abode for all.
Carrying over 30 wines by the glass and 500 bottles, it's difficult for guests
not to linger for hours on end. Especially with the "sommakase," a chef's
choice tasting menu of vino. It all begins with a few tastes of different
vintages, which inevitably turns into a bottle, and the rabbit hole of Old-
and New-World producers finally ends with the teeter-tottering of clumsy
grateful hugs and jubilant farewells. A perfect night, really.

# LOVE ADORNED

*Artisan jewelry shop*

**269 Elizabeth Street (near East Houston Street)** / **+1 212 431 5683**
**loveadorned.com** / **Open daily**

My favorite nursery rhyme has always been the one about the fine lady
atop a white horse with "rings on her fingers and bells on her toes".
From that to my mother's armfuls of silver bangles, to the Persian
necklaces I admired as a pre-teen on '70s singers, my definition of great
jewelry is a little bohemian. Love Adorned in Nolita has my number.
The shop is a fantasyland, with trays and trays of gold and silver trinkets
that are modern, a little bit country, and very rock and roll – detailed,
very well made and not even a little precious. Pile it on and you're sure
to have music wherever you go.

# MICHELE VARIAN

*Sleek Edwardian home décor*

**27 Howard Street (near Lafayette Street)** / **+1 212 343 0033**
**michelevarian.com** / **Open daily**

Some say the best gifts often come in small packages. At Michele Varian,
the best little knickknacks and home décor come in all sizes, and, most
importantly, always fit the bill, for homes of all sizes. Michele Varian,
textile designer cum boutique owner, sells handmade pillows reminiscent
of Edwardian times as well as tiny, ornate and playful trinkets that will
charm anyone, even the hardened New Yorker who normally insists on
Feng Shui-ing the crap out of all items pre-purchase. Her wallpaper line,
whichshe ingeniously sells in triple rolls, will enhance any home, whether
it's 150 square feet or 4,500 square feet.

# WARM

*Surf style for the city*

**181 Mott Street (near Kenmare Street)** / **+1 212 925 1200**
**warmny.com** / **Open daily**

Imagine you're at the beach: you throw on a flimsy dress over your favorite crocheted bikini, smooth on some coconut oil, and slip your toes into embroidered huaraches. On your way out the door, you grab a woven bag stuffed with a colorful shawl and a good book, as well as your daughter's favorite sundress and stuffed animal. OK, now imagine all the same things, only instead of walking out onto sand, you're in the middle of New York. Feels a lot easier to face the city now, right? And surely there's a rooftop pool waiting for you somewhere. At Warm, island life is a moveable feast, and they've got all the goods to make the urban jungle your personal paradise.

## BA XUYÊN
4222 8th Avenue (near 43rd Street; Sunset Park)
+1 718 633 6601, no website, open daily

## BUVETTE
42 Grove Street (near Bleecker Street; West Village)
+1 212 255 3590, ilovebuvette.com, open daily

## COSMÉ
35 East 21st Street (near Park Avenue South;
Flatiron District), +1 212 913 9659, cosmenyc.com
weekend brunch, 11:30am-2:30pm

## DIMES
49 Canal Street (near Orchard Street; Chinatown)
+1 212 925 1300, dimesnyc.com, open daily

## LE COUCOU
138 Lafayette Street (near Howard Street; SoHo)
+1 212 271 4252, lecoucou.com, weekend brunch, 10am-2pm

## ORIENTAL GARDEN
14 Elizabeth Street (near Bayard Street; Chinatown)
+1 212 619 0085, orientalgardenny.com, open daily

# best brunches in nyc

*Where weekenders recoup*

Act 1, Scene 1: After a night of debauchery, we wake to find ourselves clutching an aspirin bottle with regret lurking close by. Cut to the hair of the dog that is brunch. Grabbing an egg and cheese from a bodega may seem S.O.P. in one's hangover cure regime, but here are a few specialty brunch alternatives.

Instead of immediately going for **Buvette**'s delicious Nutella crepes or chicken salad, try their waffle sandwich – the combo of sunny-side-up egg, bacon and Gruyère topped with maple syrup has garnered a cult following.

A health nut friend suggested **Dimes** and an immediate wave of skepticism drowned out the possibility that an açaí bowl or smoked trout hash sprinkled with pomegranate seeds could cure my headache. Maybe it was the coffee with homemade almond milk or the extra sides of delicious pickled salmon, but it worked.

For something very civilized, nearby **Le Coucou** is run by Paris's most celebrated American chef, Daniel Rose. All zee accolades have made reserving an evening table in this tranquil dining room a gotta-know-people situation. Thankfully, many dinner items, including the salade de homard with sauce lauris (lobster tail, basil, tomato and a creamy, paprika-spiced sauce) are featured at brunch.

Over in the Flatiron District is **Cosmé**, a Mexican-inspired joint where the bar team concocts the most addicting sauce for their homemade micheladas. By round four, you'll be ordering extra helpings of chilaquiles, duck enmoladas and beautifully plated Nopal cactus salad.

Looking for something from the Eastern Hemisphere? Check out **Oriental Garden**, where dollies swim around the community tables offering fresh seafood and flaky egg-custard tarts. Craving savory in Brooklyn? Head to **Ba Xuyên** for Vietnamese pho – which is traditionally served in the morning – and get your salt fix with hot soup, an avocado shake and a colossal bánh mì that can easily be shared.

# midtown

## chelsea, greenwich village

Midtown West encapsulates such famous enclaves as Hell's Kitchen, the Theater District and Times Square, full of hole-in-the-walls with international flavor, Broadway babies and gawking tourists. Murray Hill in Midtown East is largely residential, nestled amidst notable landmarks the Empire State Building, Grand Central Station and Bryant Park. Korea Way, west of Murray Hill, is a street with nocturnal electric energy, and home to 24-hour karaoke bars, Korean barbecue joints and regrettable soju intoxication (you've been warned). A bit farther south is glamorous Chelsea, where art opening evenings see aficionados parading through galleries and the High Line attracts folks with its manicured grass and elevated view of the Hudson River. Hit the oh-so charming cobblestone streets of Greenwich Village to explore the small boutiques and quaint cafés. A few more steps toward the West Village and you'll discover a labyrinth of hidden gems along Cornelia Street.

1 Aedes des Venustas Perfumery
2 Bosie Tea Parlor
3 Café China
4 Chennai Garden by
  Tiffin Wallah (off map)
5 Gazala's Place
6 Metalliferous
7 Nepenthes
8 Sockerbit
9 Story (off map)
10 Tehuitzingo Mexican
  Deli & Taqueria
11 The End of History

GREENWICH VILLAGE

# AEDES PERFUMERY

*Luxury and elusive fragrances*

**7 Greenwich Avenue (near Christopher Street) / +1 212 206 8674**
**aedes.com / Open daily**

During an extensive backpacking trip in Olympic National Park, I developed
a (bad) habit of collecting pine needles and hoarding them everywhere:
my back pocket, in the tent, in my hair. I'm sure any ranger reading this
is tsk-ing from their outpost, but the scent was intoxicating. After my
trip, I went straight to Aedes Perfumery. They have an extensive selection
created by perfumers from Grasse, France, as well as a signature line
featuring lovely bottles of scents, purse sprays and candles. Don't let the
luxury brand names, chandelier and royal purple décor deter you. I went in
wearing my biking gear and said, "I'm looking for high-alpine Douglas fir
in a bottle." Within minutes the incredibly knowledgeable sales assistants
were showing me options from lines with both high and low price tags.
I'm pleased to say my months-old pine needles lay dry on my dresser next
to my carefully selected perfume bottle, and they both smell spectacular.

# BOSIE TEA PARLOR

*Afternoon refreshment and treats*

**10 Morton Street (near Bleecker Street) / +1 212 352 9900**
**bosieteaparlor.com / Open daily**

Take a French, fourth-generation pastry chef, put him in a cozy gem of a West Village space, add an extensive tea collection, and voilà: a winning result. Bosie is a cool haven in the summer, when a matcha green tea éclair is just the right sweet treat. In snowstorms, a mug of almond tea and the best canelé in town warm me to my toes. When guests are in town, I insist on taking them here for the tea service that comes complete with mini cucumber and egg salad sandwiches (crusts removed, naturally). If you go, give me a nod; I'll be the girl in the corner ogling a pile of pastry.

# CAFÉ CHINA

*Sichuan cuisine in a 1930s Shanghai setting*

**13 East 37th Street (near Madison Avenue)** / **+1 212 213 2810**
cafechinanyc.com / Open daily

Chinese expats Xian Zhang and his wife Yiming Wang understand the
transportive abilities of a restaurant. At Café China, the magic happens
before the first bite. From the moment you sidle up to the mirrored
Art Deco bar and order a cocktail by the name of Lust/Caution, you're in
their version of glamorous pre-war Shanghai. The drinks and atmosphere
are stylish enough for this to be solely a cocktail destination, but it would
be a crime to miss the food. It's Sichuan to be reckoned with: riotous
flavors, numbing peppercorns, and a mapo tofu that rivals any other.
In the snarl of Midtown East, Café China is nothing short of a miracle.

# CHENNAI GARDEN
# BY TIFFIN WALLAH

*Bombay-style vegetarian cuisine*

**127 East 28th Street (near Lexington Avenue)** / **+1 212 685 7301**
**tiffindelivery.us** / **Open daily**

I'm a bit wary of buffets – too often the food is coagulated in the chafing
tray and smells suspiciously like airplane food. I don't mean to sound
hoity-toity, but an all-you-can-eat special can be like playing Russian
roulette, where the loser wins food poisoning. Lunch here, on the other
hand, is far from this paranoid misconception. Helpful servers peek
over diner's shoulders and offer ten different condiments for a chapati.
The always-smiling head chef, Y.N. Moortho, stands proudly behind his
trays of fragrant, Bombay-style cuisine. My only concern is whether he has
replenished the depleted dosas by the time I'm ready for that third helping.

# GAZALA'S PLACE

*Druze fare from the motherland*

**709 9th Avenue (near West 49th Street)**
**+1 212 245 0709** / **facebook.com/Gazalas**
**Open daily**

Gazala's Place, one of those classic New York hallway restaurants, is short on space but its food is so delicious that it occupies a huge piece of real estate in my pantheon of eateries. It's also one of those uber-regional specialists that introduced me to the subtle difference between "Middle Eastern" general and Druze cuisine specifically. Druze food is all about flatbread, not to be confused with pita. Bowls of hummus, labneh (cheese made of strained goat milk) dusted with *za'atar* spice, fish grilled whole with lemon: all are best eaten with pieces ripped from the large, thin rounds of fermented bread served warm when you sit down. As you leave, don't forget to buy a börek or five for lunch tomorrow; you won't be sorry.

# METALLIFEROUS

*Ultimate jewelry supply*

3rd Floor, 34 West 46th Street (near 6th Avenue) / +1 212 944 0909
metalliferous.com / Closed Saturday and Sunday

As a delusional eight-year-old I thought I could pull a Steve Jobs at my parents' yard sale selling handmade jewelry. Unfortunately my octogenarian neighbors didn't exchange their social security nickels for my florescent-beaded earrings. I may have misinterpreted my cash flow forecast, but I regret more so that a Metalliferous didn't exist in my cul-de-sac. This small store carries over 30,000 base metal materials, new and vintage beads, and tools. It is the one-stop shop where sculptors, jewelry designers and novice hobbyists come to gather what they need to make their art. Time to reopen the jewelry stand...

# NEPENTHES

*Americana craftsmanship meets Japanese design*

**307 West 38th Street (near 8th Avenue)** / **+1 212 643 9540**
**nepenthesny.com** / **Open daily**

Against the cacophony within the concrete canyon of Hell's Kitchen,
Nepenthes stands cooly like a quiet wallflower. Its name carries two
meanings: the literal Japanese translation is what manager Abdul Abasi
describes as "a drug that cures all woes". The homonym is the name of
a carnivorous plant. Both meanings elicit truth. Much like for the prey
lured by a Venus flytrap's pheromone, once you enter it's difficult to leave.
The showroom itself could cure the deepest melancholia. Engineered
Garments, the Japanese-based brand stocked at Nepenthes, is made in
NYC's Garment District. Even the most discerning shopper will admire the
industrious, strong seams, and be reminded of what "Made in America"
once stood for.

# SOCKERBIT

*Swedish imports and specialty licorice*

**89 Christopher Street (near Bleecker Street)** / **+1 212 206 8170**
**sockerbit.com** / **Open daily**

My dentist once facetiously censured my guilty pleasure diet (e.g., potato chips and licorice) stating that I possessed the dental record of an 80-year-old before nonchalantly acquainting me with my retribution. Sockerbit, meaning "sugar cube," is a Scandinavian candy store in the Village that sells sweets by the pound. Carrying 150 different types of candy flavors, many sans artificial flavoring, they also offer imports such as lingonberry jam and elderflower syrup. This may be a dentist's worst nightmare, but to the incorrigible sweet tooth it warrants extra candy in one hand and dental floss in the other.

Greven

# STORY

*Virtual magazine meets retail*

**144 10th Avenue (at West 19th Street) / +1 212 242 4853**
**thisisstory.com / Closed Monday**

If one could ever physically walk along the lines and sidebars of a print magazine, Story would be the place to do it. Not only does it house a gallery and the editorial writings on the wall, it also stocks local merchandise and it practices philanthropy. This ambidextrous retail store can be mistaken for a pop-up shop, but between Story's printed words there's a longer tale to tell. Owner Rachel Shechtman has curated 12 different themes since Story's launch, all of which read like an art exhibition, editorial calendar and community outreach program rolled into one.

# TEHUITZINGO MEXICAN DELI & TAQUERIA

*Taco joint in the back of a bodega*

**695 10th Avenue (near 47th Street)** / **+1 212 397 5956**
**tehuitzingo.net** / **Open daily**

I heard about Tehuitzingo long before I set foot in it, only no one could remember the name. Someone would ask, "Have you been to that taco spot in the bodega?" Others would vaguely mention "the best Mexican in the city, over on 10th". The finally found it when I smelled delicious food coming from the office next to mine, and begged my coworker to tell me where they got it: "You know, that weird taco place in the grocery store." Some next-level Googling led me to the best goat tacos this side of the border – and yes, it's hidden inside a Mexican grocery, so you can pick up other goodies for later.

# THE END OF HISTORY

*World's largest array of vintage glass*

548 1/2 Hudson Street (at Perry Street) / +1 212 647 7598
theendofhistoryshop.blogspot.com / Open daily

Walking into this compact showroom of delicate collectibles prompts
the fear of turning into that accident-prone caricature who shatters
everything in sight. But not to worry, because owner Stephen Saunders
makes great use of the limited shelving space, carefully displaying
obscure pieces such as French opaline apothecary jars, Italian glass urns
and hand-cut porcelain vases. With its specialty in vintage hand-blown
glass, ceramics and porcelain housewares, what's old is new again at
The End of History. There's nothing like traveling back in time and
imagining past interiors in which these elegant pieces once resided.
It makes one want to dismiss today's disposable-everything and
possess such treasures once again.

# museums and galleries

*Niche miscellanies and installation art*

History whispers to you from every hallway of **The Morgan Library and Museum**. J.P. Morgan's personal collection of rarities and originals includes artifacts such as Mozart's original, hand-quilled scores, Hemingway's ornery correspondence and the Sforza family tarot cards from 1490.

Even before I moved to New York, I felt entranced by **Neue Galerie**, which shows prominent 20th-century Austrian and German art and includes an expansive collection of bewitching watercolors and sketches by Egon Schiele. Situated on Museum Mile, it's easy to pass by Neue Galerie, but be sure to look out for it.

Overlooking the Hudson River **The Cloisters** holds over 5,000 medieval European works, including the famed Unicorn Tapestries. Stained glass and gold triplychs extend throughout the rooms, underpinning the ecclesiastical aura that resonates within the monastery.

Although SoHo is now known for shopping, glimpses of its artistic, bohemian past remain. On the second floor of a 3,600-square-foot loft is **Walter De Maria's** ***The New York Earth Room***, a sculpture consisting of 280,000 pounds of lush soil, lying 22-inches deep.

Since 2004, co-owners of **Reena Spaulings Fine Art** Emily Sundblad and John Kelsey have shown fine art in the LES. The gallery focuses on international critical and conceptual art from artists who've never shown in an NYC gallery. What feels underground is certainly understated, and is a definite stop when gallery hopping in the LES.

In Queens, the eponymous **Noguchi Museum** was designed and created by the Japanese-American sculptor to display his own works. The adjoining sculpture garden is a magical place that resets buzzing creative minds with its calming, basalt stone carvings.

### NEUE GALERIE
1048 Fifth Avenue (at East 86th Street; Upper East Side), +1 212 994 9493, neuegalerie.org
closed Tuesday and Wednesday

### NOGUCHI MUSEUM
9-01 33rd Road (near Vernon Boulevard; Astoria)
+1 718 204 7088, noguchi.org
closed Monday and Tuesday

### REENA SPAULINGS FINE ART
2nd Floor, 165 East Broadway (at Rutgers Street; Lower East Side), +1 212 477 5006
reenaspaulings.com, open Thursday through Sunday

### THE CLOISTERS
99 Margaret Corbin Drive (Fort Tryon Park; Inwood)
+1 212 923 3700, metmuseum.org/visit/visit-the-cloisters, open daily

### THE MORGAN LIBRARY AND MUSEUM
225 Madison Avenue (at 36th Street; Midtown East)
+1 212 685 0008, themorgan.org, closed Monday

### WALTER DE MARIA, THE NEW YORK EARTH ROOM
141 Wooster Street (near West Houston Street; SoHo)
+1 212 989 5566, diaart.org
open Wednesday-Sunday

THE CLOISTERS

# upper west side and upper east side

## harlem, morningside heights

Notable for its music culture, the Upper West Side begins near Columbus Circle and cradles Central Park from West 59th to 110th Streets. John Lennon devotees visit the Strawberry Fields Memorial across from his former home, and near Lincoln Center, luxurious meals satiate those donning opera gloves or ostentatious outfits during Fashion Week. The Upper East Side has a prim and restrained scene – the dogs being walked seem to pick up after themselves. Beaux Arts-style mansions with built-in elevators pipe all along Madison Avenue. East of Central Park, The Neue Gallery, The Metropolitan Museum and the Guggenheim showcase some of the world's greatest art. West of Lenox Avenue, live Puerto Rican music echoes from Spanish Harlem (aka El Barrio) and locals flock to Harlem proper for juicy fried chicken and old jazz standards Despite the recent sprouting of corporate suburbia, Harlem maintains its heritage of Renaissance Revival architecture and gospel brunch on Sunday.

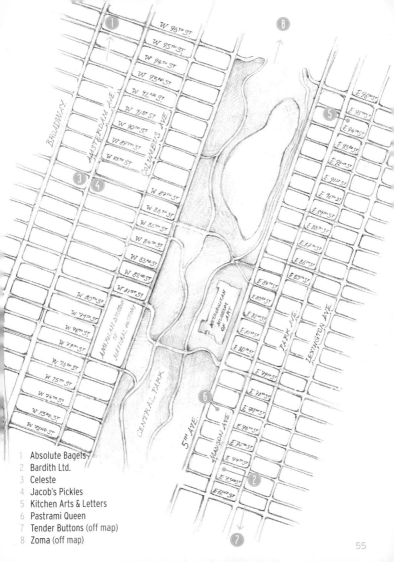

1  Absolute Bagels
2  Bardith Ltd.
3  Celeste
4  Jacob's Pickles
5  Kitchen Arts & Letters
6  Pastrami Queen
7  Tender Buttons (off map)
8  Zoma (off map)

# ABSOLUTE BAGELS

*Quintessential NYC eats*

**2788 Broadway (near West 108th Street)** / **+1 212 932 2052**
**No website** / **Open daily**

There's a line here at 6am — on a Monday. How is this possible, you ask?
For starters, Absolute Bagels (which is, fun fact, run by a Thai family) is
one of the few remaining classic joints serving hand-rolled, freshly boiled
bagels. Though it isn't the fanciest of places, the offerings have evolved
from only plain cream cheese on sesame to an everything with olive and
pimento schmear. Bagels are so fresh here they don't have to even toast
these suckers — your pick always arrives piping hot, providing a nice crunch
from its thin, glossy coating and a generous chew, so when I went on auto-
pilot and requested my cinnamon raisin toasted, I immediately cowered
with regret. Luckily, they took it in stride.

# BARDITH LTD.

*18th-century English porcelain and pottery*

**901 Madison Avenue (near East 72nd Street)** / **+1 212 737 3775**
**bardith.com** / **Closed Sunday**

Feeling like the quite literal bull in a china shop, I spent a few minutes in
Bardith Ltd. terrified I would break everything, until I relaxed and started
really seeing what was on the closely packed shelves around me. More
museum than shop, the china spans centuries and continents, all of
the quality that can make an antiques lover weep. They ship all over the
world to collectors, but if you don't have hundreds to spend on exquisite
examples of British bone china, it's a treasure trove for inspiration alone.
Whether you're a clothing designer, illustrator, or just plain interested, the
intricate patterns and unusual color palettes are sure to play muse to your
inner artist.

# CELESTE

*Little Naples in the city*

**502 Amsterdam Avenue (near West 84th Street)** / **+1 212 874 4559**
**celestenewyork.com** / **Open daily**

Walking into Celeste feels like returning to an old friend's dining room. Owner Carmine, with his towering height and stoic demeanor, welcomes the line of regulars by a nod of approval. Celeste shares Neapolitan-style home cooking using minimal, fresh ingredients. This includes an impressive menu of obscure Italian cheeses. Listen carefully as Carmine recites the list at gunshot speed, offering an extensive flavor profile and bovine history for each. The aroma of sautéed mussels and pan-seared chicken livers makes it difficult to stick to the original intention of ordering a stellar hand-tossed, wood-fired pizza. After one visit you'll want to return, knowing you'll probably get a venerable nod along with your satisfied stomach.

# JACOB'S PICKLES

*Southern accented eats*

**509 Amsterdam Avenue (near West 85th Street)**
**+1 212 470 5566 / jacobspickles.com / Open daily**

Everyone knows NYC never sleeps. But Jacob's Pickles is a real soul-food gem for night owls. Here, waiters graciously plate up toothsome brine-based comfort food until 4am, for weary service industry folk and the young office crowd alike. Owner Jacob Hadjigeorgis is passionate about his craft. Delicate flights of crisp pickles are treated as if plating caviar. White Lily flour is shipped from the South to make sure the biscuits meet texture standards. Marvelous microbrews are always on tap. A distinguished balance in acidity, sweetness and richness makes it almost too easy to forget about personal food hang-ups: it never takes long to find a way to rationalize that order of deep-fried Oreos.

# KITCHEN ARTS & LETTERS

*New and out-of-print cookbooks*

**1435 Lexington Avenue (near East 94th Street) / +1 212 876 5550**
**kitchenartsandletters.com / Closed Sunday**

Admittedly, buying a copy of Yann Duytsche's *Sweet Diversions* when I possess only a manual whisk is akin to buying $1,200 Louboutin's when training for a triathlon. But like shoes, there are some things a girl has to have. Depending on tastes and cooking know-how, staff at Kitchen Arts & Letters (who are more like seasoned librarians), prescribe the best books of culinary lore. Cataloged by subject, there are even copies of niche periodicals, such as *FOOL* from Sweden and *Apicius* from Spain, in limited numbers. So whether you want to learn Medieval Arab cookery or revisit Elizabeth David's memoir, you'll find the perfect recipe to satiate any kitchen curiosity.

# PASTRAMI QUEEN

*Sandwich royalty*

**1125 Lexington Avenue (at East 78th Street)** / **+1 212 734 1500**
**pastramiqueen.com** / **Open daily**

Like the Empire State Building, Central Park and angry taxi drivers, some things just belong to NYC. My favorite icon? Pastrami on thin-sliced rye with lots of mustard, and no one does it better than the Queen. Sure, there are other places more famous, but the first time I bit into the huge, meltingly fatty specimen here, I pledged my allegiance to this sandwich and I've never had reason to question that in all the years since. Yet, if perfect pastrami isn't enough for you, here's the bonus round: the matzoh ball soup will cure what ails you, and then some.

# TENDER BUTTONS

*Historic, artful fastenings collection*

143 East 62nd Street (near Lexington Avenue) / +1 212 758 7004
tenderbuttons-nyc.com / Closed Sunday

Since the Bronze Age, buttons have always been more than fiddly fasteners. These tiny medallions of treasure have always been representations of wealth for their wearers, works of art for their creators and keepsakes for their collectors. Today, with Martha Stewart pitching ideas of using orphan buttons as earring studs or greeting card embellishments, buttons of all sizes and vintages are sought out by crafters and tailors. Forgo NYC's Garment District and head straight to this quaint brick house in the Upper East Side, which carries buttons from 18th-century Wedgwood to porcelain China, collected from all over the world since 1964.

# ZOMA

*Bright and fresh Ethiopian cuisine*

**2084 Frederick Douglass Boulevard (at 113th Street)**
**+1 212 662 0620 / zomanyc.com / Open daily**

There's a scene in an episode of *The Simpsons* where Marge tries Ethiopian food for the first time, with great trepidation. The flavors transform her tongue into a disco floor, complete with a glitter ball, Ethiopian music and trippy Marge-shaped dancing taste buds. Watching, I immediately craved a huge platter of berbere-spiced lentils and turmeric-dyed veggies. So, I decided to make the trek up to Harlem for Zoma. I can't claim to be an expert on injera (sourdough flatbread) or doro wat (a chicken curry), but there was definitely dancing in my mouth, which I complemented with a big glass of honey wine. And just like that Simpsons episode, there was enough food for leftovers. Art inspires life, indeed.

# the other little italy

*Authenticity in The Bronx*

Though Manhattan's Little Italy has its draws, it can feel like a tourist trap at times. For those of you who want to avoid the hordes vying for a table, hop on the subway and head (way) uptown – to the Belmont section of The Bronx. This tight-knit, throwback of a community is a northern borough gem, filled with authentic restaurants, pasticcerias, meat markets, specialty grocers, beer gardens, beauty supply shops and lots of attitude. You might feel as if you've walked onto the set of *The Sopranos*, but isn't that what you want when you visit Little Italy?

With so many multigenerational families specializing in baking the same cookies, breads and wedding cakes within a four-block radius, it might be difficult to choose which one to visit. At **Gino's Pastry Shop**, there's always an enticing display of fresh nougat, sfogliatelle and pignoli. Step inside and notice (aside from dozens of framed photos of regulars and locals like Joe Pesci and Al Pacino) the several deli trays of perfectly fried cannoli shells waiting to be filled. So before going all crazy buying biscotti Regina by the pound, make sure to save space for these delicate crunchy shells, filled to order with silky smooth fresh ricotta or fluffy Bavarian cream.

When I come across a specialty shop that focuses on one thing, I know that most likely means they've honed it to a tee. **Calabria Pork Store** is one of these places, and though they may appear more like salami hoarders (sausages of various varieties dangle freely from every inch of the ceiling), they happen to specialize in curing sausages exceedingly well. As much as the 'nduja, hot flat sopressata and finocchiona sneak the spotlight, there are countless other Old-World specialties, like caciocavallo cheese, that steal the deli case spotlight. The lively atmosphere of local regulars punctuating extra syllables with heavy accents when bellowing their orders only adds to the appeal.

At **Tra Di Noi**, chef-owner Marco Coletta serves classic dishes from pollo alla cacciatora to cozze marechiaro. But we need to talk about the red sauce: it's rich with layers of sweetness and just the right amount of acidity. Though you and yours may fight over the last slice of warm, fluffy Italian bread to sop up any remaining sauce, I implore you to save room for the remaining generously portioned courses to come.

The frenetic energy and zeal of shoppers at teeny **Casa Della Mozzarella** makes it seem as if every day is the day before Thanksgiving. There's no doubt that they will run out of their silky, hand-pulled mozzarella. The bocconcini (morsels of mozzarella balls) is so addicting, you'll find yourself pulling another queue ticket for a line that is now wrapped around the block.

---

### CALABRIA PORK STORE
2338 Arthur Avenue (near East 186th Street;
Belmont), +1 718 367 5145
facebook.com/CalabriaPorkStoreBx, open daily

### CASA DELLA MOZZARELLA
604 East 187th Street
(near Arthur Avenue; Belmont), +1 718 364 3867
facebook.com/CasaDellaMozzarella, open daily

### GINO'S PASTRY SHOP
580 East 187th Street (near Hoffman Street;
Belmont), +1 718 584 3558
facebook.com/cannoliking60, closed Monday

### TRA DI NOI
622 East 187th Street (near Hughes Avenue;
Belmont), +1 718 295 1784, tradinoi.com
closed Monday

# red hook and gowanus

## boerum hill, carroll gardens

You've got to admire the tenacity of the residents and business owners of these South Brooklyn neighborhoods, who rebuilt their lives after the battering 13-foot-high waves unleashed by Hurricane Sandy in 2012. Red Hook, named for the color of its soil, is best visited by water taxi, which allows for picture-perfect skyline views including, of course, the lady herself, The Statue of Liberty. Eastward is Gowanus, a neighborhood known for its industrial setting and alleged mobster-related corpses that purportedly float in the Gowanus Canal. Despite the grisly allegations, the serene residential nooks along Smith Street and charming eateries along 3rd Avenue are definitely not to be missed.

Map labels:

- PACIFIC ST
- DEAN ST
- BERGEN ST
- WYCKOFF ST
- WARREN ST
- BALTIC ST
- BUTLER ST
- DOUGLASS ST
- DEGRAW ST
- SACKETT ST
- UNION ST
- HENRY ST
- 2ND PL
- CLINTON ST
- COURT ST
- SMITH ST
- HOYT ST
- BOND ST
- NEVINS ST
- 3RD AVE
- UNION ST
- PRESIDENT ST
- CARROLL ST
- 1ST ST
- 3RD ST
- 6TH ST
- 7TH ST
- 8TH ST
- 2ND AVE
- 9TH ST
- 10TH ST
- 3RD AVE
- LORRAINE ST
- BAY ST

1 Erie Basin (off map)
2 Hometown Bar-B-Que (off map)
3 Littleneck
4 Rucola
5 Shelsky's of Brooklyn
6 The Brooklyn Circus

67

# ERIE BASIN

*Eclectic vintage and antique jewelry*

**388 Van Brunt Street (at Dikeman Street)** / **+1 718 554 6147**
**eriebasin.com** / **Open Wednesday through Saturday**

For the past decade, this treasure of a boutique has sat in the bowels of Red Hook, where neighboring buildings share the same weathered, striking patina as the 18th-century jewelry (including a line of engagement rings) and Victorian tokens housed within this small, homely gallery. Each object is carefully distinguished, passionately curated and extremely reasonably priced. Owner Russell Whitmore, though quiet and reserved, is most eager to tell you the backstory of every one-of-a-kind piece. But, just when clients start fishing for their wallets, Whitmore, like clockwork, compulsively spills the last-minute beans, sharing the most miniscule flaws not caught by the typical eye so that the customer knows exactly what they're buying. This transparency and trust is exactly the reason why I return each time to fog up the windows, hear stories and cross my fingers they'll still remain upon my next visit.

# HOMETOWN
# BAR-B-QUE

*The United Nations of smokehouse specialties*

**454 Van Brunt Street (at Reed Street) / +1 347 294 4644**
**hometownbarbque.com / Closed Monday**

Pitmaster and owner Billy Durney has certainly cultivated the most diplomatic and vibrant menu – it's able to bring (literally) everyone together. When asked what style of barbecue he serves, Durney states that it's "Brooklyn," though, when you look at the menu, it's apparent that his joint comprises numerous meats cooked in various styles of preparations that highlight and reflect the diverse culture that is New York. Texas-style brisket that can take up to 18-plus hours to prepare, Vietnamese hot wings, lamb belly bánh mì, Chinese sticky ribs, Jamaican jerk baby back ribs and handmade tortillas for pulled pork tacos can all be found under one roof. Many may argue that barbecue should be simple, and Durney has learned to prove that theory with the brisket sandwich. Tender morsels of beef and its decadent drippings are cushioned next to crunchy pickles and onions, all within a pillowy roll.

# LITTLENECK

*Lobster rolls for the seafarer*

**288 3rd Avenue (near Carroll Street)** / **+1 718 522 1921**
**littleneckbrooklyn.com** / **Closed Tuesday**

If there was ever a lobster roll eating contest, I'd walk home with a dozen blue ribbons — especially if it were held at Littleneck. The lobster here has just the right amount of aioli, zing and sweetness, all enveloped in a little buttery bun that stays crisp to the last bite of juicy meat. The restaurant surrounds seafood lovers with a quaint nautical theme that evokes the scent of New England's sea air. Perhaps the competition comes at the end of the seafood feast, in seeing who has enough room left to do justice to a slice of locally made pie from The Blue Stove bakery.

# RUCOLA

*Northern Italian farm to table*

**190 Dean Street (at Bond Street)** / **+1 718 576 3209**
**rucolabrooklyn.com** / **Open daily**

Tucked away inside a handsome corner brownstone, Rucola's diners
gravitate to its center communal table and are transported to a pastoral
Piemonte scene, where aromas of fresh herbs and white truffles dominate.
It's the ultimate neighborhood gem, serving up bountiful grilled goodies
and taking every opportunity to turn a simple gathering into a joyous
celebration. To find this centerpiece of old-world Italian in historic Brooklyn,
look out for its romantic wrought-iron façade with a prolific array of
verdant foliage.

# SHELSKY'S OF BROOKLYN

*Old-school Jewish delicatessen*

**141 Court Street (near Atlantic Avenue)** / **+1 718 855 8817**
**shelskys.com** / **Open daily**

I once lived on the West Coast and deemed it "best coast" due to its
abundance of fresh, Pacific seafood. But when it comes to cured fish,
New York reigns legendary. Owner Peter Shelsky keeps it local, carrying
produce from Brooklyn's cure kings ACME Smoked Fish as well as The
Smokehouse in Mamaroneck, while bagels and bialys come from Lower
East Side's Kossar's and Davidivitch in Queens. What better bagels to
envelope layers of silky lox and smooth, dense cream cheese? Peter's very
own whitefish salad, folded together with rich mayonnaise and crunchy,
house-pickled cucumbers, is so addictive, just pray there's room in your
carry-on to show West Coasters what's up.

# THE BROOKLYN CIRCUS

*Vintage Americana*

**150 Nevins Street (near Bergen Street) / +1 718 858 0919**
**thebkcircus.com / Closed Monday**

Lauded as being a fashion visionary, store owner Ouigi Theodore has proven that looking back to the past is a way of moving forward in fashion. Whether it's the Harlem Renaissance or the Civil Rights Movement, fashion finds references from history's landscape. Ouigi's inspirations range from his Haitian roots, to NYC culture, Marcus Garvey and *The Cosby Show*, and these are all incorporated into the store's emphasis on vintage. Having grown up playing baseball and varsity football, a strong collegiate, athletic slant can be seen in his sportswear and expertly tailored casual clothes. With fashion always evolving, Ouigi's philosophy of a constant editing eye for reinvention is what has allowed The Brooklyn Circus to transcend trends for so many years.

# graffiti masterpieces

*Vivid storytellers*

Its ink may seem permanent, but New York street art is transient. Whether it's the cryptic epigrams of SAMO© artist and Warhol-collaborator Jean-Michel Basquiat in the LES; Cost & Revs's obscure wheat-pasting exploits; or crochet street artist Olek; graffiti inevitably gets replaced with, at best, something equally inspired or, at worst, by gentrified high-rise condos.

Thankfully, countless legendary local and international artists continue to voice out and transform dilapidated brick walls into colorful manifestos. Head east from Williamsburg to find **The Bushwick Collective**, an outdoor gallery in an industrial warehouse area. It sustains the now defunct 5Pointz Aerosol Art Center's philosophy of uniting street artists from the five boroughs with their brethren all over the world. You'll see signature styles from locals Joe Lurato, Buff Monster and Jerkface here.

In Manhattan, 5Pointz founder Jonathan Cohen, aka Meres One, has found a new canvas on **Rag & Bone's Wall**. Over at Houston and Bowery, **The Bowery Mural** – the spot that hosted Keith Haring's famous work in 1982 – has turned into a sanctioned outdoor exhibition space that is constantly updated with new works from different artists.

Two original **Keith Haring** exterior murals remain today, one at the Carmine outdoor swimming pool in Greenwich Village and the other in East Harlem. While near East Harlem, make sure to also check out the latest paintings at **Graffiti Hall of Fame**. Back in Chelsea, their oversized cousins tower over **The High Line**, from where you can see changing pieces commissioned throughout the year.

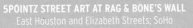

**5POINTZ STREET ART AT RAG & BONE'S WALL**
East Houston and Elizabeth Streets; SoHo

**GRAFFITI HALL OF FAME**
East 106th Street and Park Avenue; East Harlem

**KEITH HARING EXTERIOR MURALS**
*Carmine Street Swimming Pool*: Carmine Street and
7th Avenue; Greenwich Village
*Crack is Wack*: East 128th Street and 2nd Avenue;
East Harlem

**THE BOWERY MURAL**
East Houston and Bowery Streets; SoHo

**THE BUSHWICK COLLECTIVE**
Troutman Street and Saint Nicholas Avenue;
Bushwick

**THE HIGH LINE STREET ART**
529 West 20th Street; Chelsea

THE BUSHWICK COLLECTIVE

# fort greene and prospect heights

## dumbo, prospect park, vinegar hill

Hop off the Brooklyn Bridge pedestrian pathway and you'll find a queue into Brooklyn's established culinary scene. West of the Brooklyn Navy Yard and east of Dumbo (Down Under the Manhattan Bridge Overpass), Vinegar Hill is a quaint neighborhood with Greek Revival-style row houses. In Fort Greene and Prospect Heights, tree-lined streets and sport utility baby strollers elicit a slower pace compared to its northern hipster precincts. Daily joggers have Prospect Park and Brooklyn Botanical Garden, while other healthy types make beelines to the many yoga studios nearby. Within the 478-plus manicured acres of Park Slope's Green-Wood Cemetery – a national historic landmark – you'll find the highest city viewpoint in Brooklyn. Clinton Hill, with its lavish old Beaux Arts-style houses, is home to film stars and musicians as well as Barclays Center and Brooklyn Academy of Music, the oldest performing multi-arts center in the country.

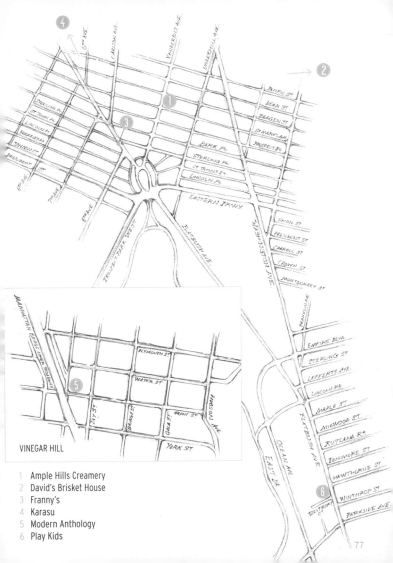

VINEGAR HILL

1   Ample Hills Creamery
2   David's Brisket House
3   Franny's
4   Karasu
5   Modern Anthology
6   Play Kids

# AMPLE HILLS CREAMERY

*Organic ice cream and classic sundae shop goodness*

**623 Vanderbilt Avenue (at St Marks Avenue)** / **+1 347 240 3926**
**amplehills.com** / **Open daily**

The weekend that Ample Hills opened, I walked by on a sweltering night around 7pm and saw a line around the corner. Thinking that the crowd was just there to cool off, I had a giggle at the name and kept moving, telling myself that a popsicle would work just as well. When I finally got to try a scoop of Ample's chocolate ice cream and another of salted caramel, I knew I had misinterpreted the reason for that line. Super fresh organic cream and bold, salt-forward swirls of flavor put this frozen goodness head and shoulders above anything you'll find in the supermarket, or in many other ice cream shops, for that matter.

# DAVID'S BRISKET HOUSE

*Bona fide pastrami sandwiches*

**533 Nostrand Avenue (near Herkimer Place)** / **+1 718 789 1155**
**davidsbriskethouseinc.com** / **Open daily**

Though I live on the same street as beloved Katz's Delicatessen,
seeing that endless line encourages me to venture elsewhere for my
briny pastrami and corned beef. Who knew a staunch standby would
be in Bedstuy (Bedford-Stuyvesant, for long). David's brisket sandwich
is layered a mile high, with a side of luxurious jus, for half the price.
If that doesn't pacify a hungry stomach or loud mouth, I don't know
what will. In a neighborhood primarily populated with West African
and fried chicken cuisine, there's still a lunch line. The only difference is,
rather than camera-frenzied tourists, you'll wait alongside locals, some
of whom have been coming here since the 1960s.

# FRANNY'S

*Greenmarket-driven neighborhood gem*

**348 Flatbush Avenue (near Sterling Place)** / **+1 718 230 0221**
**frannysbrooklyn.com** / **Open daily**

Despite being around for over a decade, this warm, wood-adorned dining room remains a clubhouse to members of a fervent fan club of highly acclaimed chefs, sommeliers, local artists and quality-obsessed locals. Though Park Slope was ground zero for gentrification and the evolution of food politics in Brooklyn, Franny's is more than trendy: its humble gratitude for fellow farmers and winemakers, and its endeavor to put one step forward for greater environmental and social change make it a mainstay. Owners Francine Stephens and Andrew Feinberg – who also run BKLYN Larder down the street – not only support local, but also invest in renewable energy like wind power. Co-chefs Ian Auger and Rikki Giambruno consistently deliver sublime housemade sausage, wood-fired pizza and the creamiest panna cotta that gleefully floats with every spoonful.

# KARASU

*Sophisticated Japanese speakeasy and restaurant*

**166 Dekalb Avenue (at Cumberland Street) / +1 347 223 4811**
**karasubk.com / Open daily**

Walk past the tables of oysters on the half shell and Americana comfort food in the dining room at Walter's Foods, pass through the back door and you'll be transported to Little Kyoto. The warm, cozy cocoon of a tatami room that is Karasu, goes way beyond a speakeasy, though the downy glow of amber lights bounce off the beautiful copper bar, accenting the aesthetic details of the all-vintage glassware. It may come off as the perfect date spot for cocktail enthusiasts, but what inevitably ends up happening is that Karasu's enticing array of mouthwatering snacks and plates will start calling your name after round four of signature cocktails like the One Flight Up (white run, green tea, lime, shiso); you'll also decide to sate your now-ravenous appetite with the koji prime ribeye for two with tosazu sauce.

# MODERN ANTHOLOGY

*Men's compendium of design*

**68 Jay Street (near Front Street)** / **+1 718 552 3020**
**modernanthology.com** / **Open daily**

Modern Anthology has an extraordinary collection of retro treasures of
form and function. A meander through the store is like simultaneously
walking through the Smithsonian and the Museum of Natural History
both at once, thanks to an array of topography maps, old-fashioned
outdoor apparatuses and furry friends in taxidermy heaven. A flashback
of childhood is found in many knickknacks, whether it's vintage dice or
filament bulbs. This boutique has an emphasis on timeless, masculine
and handsome designs, and also carries gifts of adult whimsy: Max Poglia
handmade knives, leather goods and mid-century modern furniture.

# PLAY KIDS

*Smart toys for smart kids*

**668 Flatbush Avenue (near Hawthorne Street)** / **+1 347 715 9347**
**playkidsstore.com** / **Open daily**

There once was a time when playthings were made of solid, indestructible materials. A time when kids played rough, yet at the end of the day no tears were shed over a broken wing or a missing glass eye. At Play Kids, it's the parents who step inside first, with youngsters in tow. This is no ordinary toy store. Owners Shelley Kramer and Carl Blake make it a point to carry playthings that last. They also want children to get optimal enjoyment from their products, so they offer daily workshops and events. From drum-alongs to sing-alongs, this is a place for those looking for something more than just temporal toys.

# public markets

*Locavore havens*

**BROOKLYN FLEA MARKET & SMORGASBURG**
1 Hanson Place (at Ashland Place; Fort Greene)
weekends (winter)
176 Lafayette Avenue (near Vanderbilt Avenue;
Fort Greene), open Saturday (summer)
Manhattan Bridge Archway Plaza (near Water Street;
Dumbo), open Sunday (summer)
brooklynflea.com

**CHELSEA MARKET**
75 9th Avenue (near West 16th Street; Chelsea)
chelseamarket.com, open daily

**ESSEX STREET MARKET**
120 Essex Street (near Delancey Street;
Lower East Side), +1 212 312 3603
essexstreetmarket.com, open daily

**FORT GREENE FLEA MARKET**
176 Lafayette Street (near Vanderbilt Avenue;
Fort Greene), brooklynflea.com, Saturday (summer)

Weekend afternoons in New York are filled with possibility – but a favorite past time amongst locals? Hitting up markets. Rain or shine, summer or winter, you should absolutely check out what these markets have to offer, be it incredible snacks, locally harvested produce, artisan-created furniture and threads or throwback tschotskes.

In the summer, outdoor markets are king. **Fort Greene Flea Market** and **Brooklyn Flea Market & Smorgasburg** are wildly popular with folks seeking out priceless antiques from amongst kitsch bric-a-brac, or foodies hunting the best local fare. There's also a strong sense of community between the vendors.

I prefer eating al fresco on sunny days, but in winter I escape indoors at **Brooklyn Flea Market & Smorgasburg**, in a huge 50,000-square-foot space where over 100 vendors cozy up next to 50 brick-and-mortar businesses. World-renowned for its impressive food hall, **Chelsea Market** offers cuisines ranging from bánh mì sandwiches to fresh masa tortillas, and Thai curries to ice cream from local dairy farms.

For something more traditional, the **Essex Street Market**, originally housing push-carts in the 1940s, now hosts respected vendors who've sold their prime cuts, fresh fish, cheeses, breads and tropical fruits for several generations.

FORT GREENE FLEA MARKET

# williamsburg and greenpoint

## bedford-stuyvesant, bushwick

Thousands of Lower East Side residents crossed the Williamsburg Bridge in 1903, relocating to Bedford-Stuyvesant and South and East Williamsburg. Today, folks may grimace when taking the so-called "G-eriatric" G train, which runs the longitude of Brooklyn rather than directly into Manhattan. Yet, it seems Millennials have no qualms humble-bragging about their epic commute. Once dubbed the "Third hippest neighborhood in the country" by *Forbes* magazine, the area continues to test trends and embodies a youthful energy. Despite hipster affectations, it's worth visiting Little Poland in Greenpoint for warm pierogi or doughnuts on Manhattan Avenue. Williamsburg also has some great spots for admiring the skyline of Manhattan, namely the view from the East River Ferry (see pg 126) or from Wythe Hotel's rooftop bar, The Ides (see pg 9).

1   Bakeri
2   Bellocq Tea Atelier
3   Dun-Well Doughnuts
4   Mociun
5   Moe's Doughs Donut Shop

6   Okonomi/Yuji
7   Open Air Modern
8   Oroboro
9   Pip-Squeak Chapeau Etc.
10   Stella Dallas Living

# BAKERI

*Lovingly made goods*

**150 Wythe Avenue (near North 8th Street) / +1 718 388 8037**
**bakeribrooklyn.com / Open daily**

In my dream life, in which I'm a neurosurgeon with loads of free time,
I get up at 4am to make gorgeous loaves of hand-shaped bread, platters
of frittata and baskets of muffins. I'd do all this myself because, when
it comes down to it, homemade is just better. Or so I thought until I
went to Bakeri, where my dream life and real life collided spectacularly.
This collective of cool girls make dreamy baked goods that rival grandma's.
Enjoy them in the cozy dining area, have some outside in their garden, or
take them home and pretend you made them yourself. A word to the wise:
no need to wake up pre-sunrise, but they do have a tendency to sell out,
so get there early for the best selection.

# BELLOCQ TEA ATELIER

*Leaves parfumerie*

**104 West Street (near Kent Street) / +1 347 463 9231 / bellocq.com**
**Closed Monday and Tuesday**

From the rich yolk-colored packaging, to the evocative names, to the smell and taste of the blends, the leaves at Bellocq are transportive. Inhale the White Wolf and you're wandering a winter-bright forest in Russia, all pine and snow. The Queen's Guard is floral, but the rose and lavender soften the strong backbone of the black Ceylon. What I'm addicted to, though, is the Earl Grey as I've never had it before: fresh Sicilian bergamot oil puts imitatorto shame, and it just needs a touch of cream to be an ease to any worry.

# DUN-WELL DOUGHNUTS

*Vegan donuts done well*

**222 Montrose Avenue (near Bushwick Avenue) / +1 917 555 1212 dunwelldoughnuts.com / Open daily**

Vegan isn't really in my vocabulary, but when donuts are this pillowy, with crisp exteriors and a plush crumb, who cares what's not in them? Dun-Well is all soda-shop charm meets lumberjack hipster: expect food to be served on a round of wood by a man wearing a bowtie and striped shirt. Those exemplary donuts are the main draw, but the creative duo behind this operation also whips up ice cream, soda syrups and savory snacks. And since there are no animal products to be found, feel free to convince yourself it's healthy, too.

mociun

*Scandinavian-inspired boutique*

**224 Wythe Avenue (at North 4th Street)   +1 718 387 3731**
**mociun.com   Open daily**

This storefront may be mistaken for a pristine art gallery, but look closer and you'll find Doug Johnston's chorded merchandise playfully displayed across the store's glossy cement floor, atop windowsills, underneath tables and against stark white walls. Getting down on one's knees to test out floor pillows by Shabd or the shape of Eric Bonnin's ceramics feels like visiting the minimalist abode of that stylish friend you secretly envy. That "stylish friend" is designer and storeowner Caitlin Mociun, who just so happens to seek one-of-a-kind pieces created by small, local designers; some whose studios are their kitchen tables. Mociun is a place of constant rumination, inspiration and progression.

# MOE'S DOUGHS DONUT SHOP

*Classic creations, eccentrically flavored*

**126 Nassau Avenue (near McGuinness Boulevard)** / **+1 718 349 1216**
**facebook.com/MoesDoughs** / **Open daily**

Friends, fans and family have all chided me when I insinuated that beloved
Peter Pan's Donut and Pastry Shop might not be the best in town anymore.
I'm spreading the doughnut love and, as it happens, Moe's is just around the
corner from the venerable Peter Pan's. In fact, owner Moe Saleh worked there for
18 years. He still has the magic touch — his treats are fresh, not overly sweet, light
as air and can be enjoyed at the counter. It's difficult to just eat one with such
classics as toasted coconut, red velvet and crème filled, but it's the signatures
that keep loyalists returning. The samoa (a very accurate take on the Girl Scout
cookie of the same name), doussant (the cronut's second cousin) and a rainbow-
colored old fashioned are difficult to resist. It's incredibly hard not to fill an entire
box, especially when the confections are just a little over a buck apiece.

# OKONOMI/ YUJI RAMEN

*Soup by day and noodles by night*

**150 Ainslie Street (near Lorimer Street) / +1 718 302 0598**
**okonomibk.com / Open daily**

One of the reasons why Okonomi became an instant success is that it cultivated a sanctuary for even the most harried New Yorkers to reboot and call to mind the importance of balance and harmony. Traditional ichiju-sansai (literally meaning "one soup, three dishes") offers a choice of different filets accompanied with miso soup, seven-grain rice and sides of seasonal vegetables. Whether salt roasted, marinated in saikyo miso, sake kasu or even dry kelp cured, owner Yuji Haraguchi sources daily catch from the New Fulton Fish Market in the Bronx. Yuji demonstrates mottainai — the Japanese concept of avoiding waste — within his cuisine: fish bones and vegetables go into a pot every morning in preparation for the ramen broth that will be used at night. The cyclical practice of reclaiming is expressed even in local artist Jordan Colón's ceramics made from New York soil, from which Yuji's enriched ramen broth is ladled.

# OPEN AIR MODERN

*Danish 20th-century furniture and rare books*

**489 Lorimer Street  (near Powers Street) / +1 718 383 6465**
**openairmodern.com / Closed Monday**

My love for Scandinavian design comes from my father, an architect whose
trundle beds and dining nooks look like something from a Carl Larsson
painting. From there, it was just a hop and a skip and an art major to a
full-blown obsession with all things mid-20th-century and Danish.
Open Air Modern owner Matt Singer shares my obsession and stocks
his airy rehabbed garage with mint-condition pieces. I'd love to fill my
apartment with his lust-worthy furniture, all burnished wood tones and
modern silhouettes, but while I try to save up, it's the vintage Dansk
tableware and the hard-to-find art and design books that keep me
coming back for more.

OROBORO

*A new home for bobo-chic everything*

**326 Wythe Avenue (at South 1st Street)   +1 718 388 4884**
**oroborostore.com   Open daily**

Oroboro is a whirlwind of striking mysticism and bohemian-inspired wares that gathers its silky, frayed seams with a sense of great profundity. Owner April Hughes offers a kaleidoscope of colors and textures that could transfix anyone into a dreamlike state. Womenswear is revolutionized on the hanger, as the items whisper influences of a modern-day Paul Poiret or Christian Lacroix, and the jewelry, accessories and home goods are irresistible. The birch branches intertwined with leather acting as racks paired with the whitewashed brick walls and wood flooring makes one feel as if they've stepped inside an exquisitely decorated alpinist's bungalow. Oroboro is that far-off land where, if textile alchemy existed, it would be practiced here.

# PIP-SQUEAK CHAPEAU ETC.

*Linen sophisticates*

**99 Franklin Street (near Milton Street)** / **+1 917 270 5184**
pip-squeakchapeau.com / **Closed Monday and Tuesday**

At Pip-Squeak Chapeau Etc., you'll seek comfort in the crinkling of natural fibers found in designer Sveta Kazakova's pieces. She emphasizes that clothing should be more about how one feels, rather than devoting time to fashion norms. With summer heat hitting triple digits, I wish I shared the moxie of NYC women on GoTopless Day, but I'll stick to Sveta's A-line tanks of billowing, cool linen that won't adhere to sweaty skin. Her no-frill designs exude elegance, like crow's feet formed from a gentle smile. It's the subtleties that speak for generations, and her pieces of simplicity and grace will surely last a lifetime.

# STELLA DALLAS LIVING

*Vintage textile oasis*

285 North 6th Street (near Meeker Avenue) / +1 718 387 6898
facebook.com/stelladallasnyc / Open daily

If I lived anywhere other than here, it'd probably be in a log cabin in the middle of the woods. Why? So that I could stock up on all the dreamy goods found at Stella Dallas Living and then swathe every room with Aztec blankets, pre-Colonial Amish quilts and antique German silk-woven piano covers from the turn of the century. Co-owners Mago and Junko Watanabe have been collecting heritage items that many immigrants had brought with them across the Atlantic. Beyond secondhand linens that date back to the 1830s, Stella Dallas also carries vintage fur shawls and Japanese silk kimonos in near-mint condition. This isn't your ordinary pre-loved treasure trove (although Stella Dallas's sister store 10 Ft. Single, which specializes in just that, is dangerously located next door), but it is the type of place where set dressers help win awards; fashion designers seek inspiration; and I find the perfect Italian lace doily for my dollhouse of an apartment in the Lower East Side.

## ARLENE'S GROCERY
95 Stanton Street (near Orchard Street; Lower East Side)
+1 212 358 1633, arlenesgrocery.net, open daily

## BARGEMUSIC
Fulton Ferry Landing, 1 Water Street (near Old Fulton Street; DUMBO), +1 718 624 2083, bargemusic.org
open Friday through Sunday

## BOSSA NOVA CIVIC CLUB
1271 Myrtle Avenue (near Evergreen Avenue; Bushwick)
+1 718 443 1271, bossanovacivicclub.com, open daily

## GOOD ROOM
98 Meserole Avenue (near Manhattan Avenue; Greenpoint)
+1 718 349 2373, goodroombk.com, open Wednesday through Saturday

## (LE) POISSON ROUGE
158 Bleecker Street (near Thompson Street; West Village)
+1 212 505 3474, lprnyc.com, open daily

## ROCKWOOD MUSIC HALL
196 Allen Street (near East Houston Street; Lower East Side)
+1 212 477 4155, rockwoodmusichall.com, open daily

## SMALLS JAZZ CLUB
183 West 10th Street (near West 4th Street; Greenwich Village)
+1 646 476 4346, smallslive.com, open daily

## THE BOWERY BALLROOM
6 Delancey Street (near Bowery; Nolita), +1 212 533 2111
boweryballroom.com, check website for schedule

## TRANS-PECOS
915 Wyckoff Avenue (near Hancock Street; Ridgewood)
no phone, thetranspecos.com, open daily

## VILLAGE VANGUARD
178 7th Avenue South (near Perry Street; Greenwich Village)
+1 212 255 4037, villagevanguard.com, open daily

## WARSAW
261 Driggs Avenue (near Eckford Street; Greenpoint)
+1 718 387 0505, warsawconcerts.com, check website for schedule

# live entertainment

*The Carnegie Hall alternative*

Be they divas looking to become the next Aretha or a new band whose sole release has just gone viral, this city is an epicenter for aspiring musicians. If you're interested in catching the next big thing before they get big, then shimmy your way to these venues.

Historical landmark **The Bowery Ballroom** still boasts some of its original 1930s fittings but there's nothing dated about the acoustics – the sound quality is the big draw. Singer-songwriters and rock bands are regularly discovered at cover-charge-free **Rockwood Music Hall**, and the indie crowd flocks to **Arlene's Grocery**, a former bodega turned music venue. Punk rockers should check out **Warsaw**, a Polish community center where artists like Angel Olsen and Crystal Castles have serenaded sold-out shows and instigated obligatory mosh pits.

Inside a defunct textile mill, not-for-profit venue **Trans-Pecos** hosts everyone from electronic music pundits to aspiring artists of all backgrounds. During the day, they teach DJing to underprivileged children and adults with intellectual and developmental disabilities. By night, red strobes and plumes of fog surround local DJs, and the crowd garners a strong sense of appreciation of music rather than who's-who in the room.

For those who wish to dance the night away, **Good Room** and **Bossa Nova Civic Club** are where to find the heavy bass vibrations of deep house and the hypnotic beats of acid house until the wee morning hours.

Beyond the halls of Alice Tully Hall, classical music enthusiasts can enjoy concerts at **Bargemusic**, where a floating barge takes center stage and the East River and Lower Manhattan skyline act as backdrop. Looking for contemporary classical or avant-garde sounds? Visit **(Le) Poisson Rouge**, a multimedia venue founded by musicians from the Manhattan School of Music.

Jazz is synonymous with New York, and tiny, iconic spot **Smalls Jazz Club**'s 60 seats fill up fast, so show up early. If you can't squeeze in there, make your way to **Village Vanguard**, where headlining acts have included John Coltrane and Dexter Gordon, and audience have been swoonin' and swingin' for decades.

# long island city and astoria

## woodside, sunnyside

---

Though there are five train lines that make stops in Long Island City, this neighborhood is often overlooked as a go-to destination. As home to Silvercup Studios, which cleverly sensationalizes NYC pop culture into every program it produces (*Sex in the City* and *30 Rock*, to name but two); The American Museum of the Moving Image; experimental exhibition space MoMA PS1; and art house The SPACE L.I.C., it is an epicenter for filmmakers and artists alike. There are also plenty of hidden-gem ethnic eateries that'll tempt visitors to dinner before seducing them into signing a year's lease in the neighborhood after dessert.

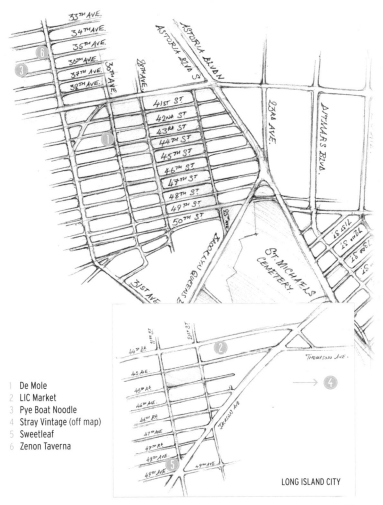

1 De Mole
2 LIC Market
3 Pye Boat Noodle
4 Stray Vintage (off map)
5 Sweetleaf
6 Zenon Taverna

LONG ISLAND CITY

# DE MOLE

*Pueblan cuisine from the home country*

**45-02 48th Avenue (at 45th Street)** / **+1 718 392 2161**
**demolenyc.com** / **Open daily**

I recall taking frequent family trips to Seoul as a kid, when my mother would check in multiple empty suitcases, zipped one within another like Russian dolls, for the sole purpose of hoarding back kombu, anchovies and squid. "It tastes better from the Korean seashore," she'd say. Like her, part owner and chef Ramiro Mendez flies back ingredients from his homeland, Santa Inés Ahuatempan, Puebla, including the impressive 17 that he uses in his robust signature mole. Truth be told, you can't go wrong when fresh ingredients are paired with passed-down family recipes. Sure, there's a time and place for the corner taqueria stand, but it can't compete when a craving for sweet and spicy mole and zippy hibiscus fresca strikes.

# LIC MARKET

*Locavore hot spot*

**21-52 44th Drive (near 23rd Street)** / **+1 718 361 0013**
**licmarket.com** / **Open daily**

LIC Market is not your typical 200-seat, cacophonous, $100-a-head
NYC restaurant. In fact, it feels like a gourmand's home. Its foyer is
converted into a diner, and the fragrant scent of herbs tickles the
senses on the walk down the hall to the eight tables in the back room.
Owner and chef Alex Schindler prepares specials every day for loyal
customers and commuters alike. Making everything fresh within a
24-hour period; carrying strictly seasonal produce; and using only
hormone- and antibiotic-free provisions, this is a place that makes
one consider becoming an official local regular.

# PYE BOAT NOODLE

*Robust Thai soups*

**35-13 Broadway (near 36th Street)**
**+1 718 685 2329 / pyeboatnoodle.com**
**Open daily**

Astoria has always been a neighborhood ripe for new brick and mortars offering foods from around the world. This is undoubtedly one of New York's most diverse neighborhoods, as cuisines within a five-block radius can range from homemade spanakopita to divine croque madames to savory ramen. Add a bowl from Pye Boat Noodle to the mix, adequately and traditionally thickened and tinged with pork blood, and you'll have vicariously traveled to Bangkok's canals and floating markets in one slurp. The broth of the tom yum "bolarn" noodle is so toothsome, it's no surprise that the condiment caddy carrying various chili accouterments is rarely touched. Here, the use of zero MSG makes for a delicate and bright flavor. Yet, if you're a sucker for salt and tang, rest easy knowing a bottle of fish sauce will land on your table with your meal.

# STRAY VINTAGE

*Treasures far from abandonment*

**4809 Skillman Avenue (near 48th Street) / +1 718 779 7795**
**strayvintage.com / Closed Monday and Tuesday**

This mid-century vintage store, housing secondhand housewares neatly laid out in organized fashion, feels like a hip grandmother's cottage. There's everything from cherry-wood chairs, to various beveled mirrors hanging along the wall, and even an assortment of reasonably priced pre-prohibition stemware. You can imagine hip grandma passing you a Manhattan in a mint-condition, etched cocktail glass. Stray Vintage is different from other secondhand stores, because there is no need for treasure "hunting" here. It's all perfectly laid out, and pieces happen to spontaneously land in one's eager grasp, each one so pristinely pretty that you just know its next home will most likely be its last.

# SWEETLEAF

*The church of coffee*

**10-93 Jackson Avenue (at 11th Street) / +1 917 832 6726**
**sweetleaflic.com / Open daily**

Every time I visit any one of Long Island City's day-trip destinations,
such as MoMA P.S. 1, I always end up at Sweetleaf. I used to think it was
the comforting ambiance of the space, or the perfectly extracted espresso
from "Dorothy", the La Marzocco Linea machine, but I've discovered it's
really the carrot cake that keeps me coming back drooling. Pastry authority
Beverly Lauchner bakes everything in-house, from the fluffy, cinnamon
and granulated sugar coated donuts to that life-changing carrot cake.
Owner Freddy stocks beans hailing from the Pacific Northwest, including
caffeine field faves Heart Coffee and Stumptown. Rejoice.

# THE BURGER GARAGE

*Quality sandwich pit stop*

25-36 Jackson Avenue (at 44th Street) / +1 718 392 0424
theburgergarage.com / Open daily

This is a burger joint for both the purist as well as for the friend who
always asks if the kitchen can "caramelize the onions". It's a place where
the helpful service staff has no qualms in adding to the long list of toppings
off the seasonal board, or adapting to dietary requirements including
gluten intolerance. Using fresh, ground meats from local celebrity butcher
Pat LaFrieda, Burger Garage doesn't skimp when forming a quarter-pound of
pure Angus Beef brisket, chuck and prime rib cuts. Caloric intake increases as
one gets into savory sautéed mushrooms and fried egg topping territory.

# ZENON TAVERNA

*Family-owned Cypriot dining room*

**34-10 31st Avenue (near 34thStreet)** / **+1 718 956 0133**
**zenontaverna.com** / **Open daily**

On this street of Astoria let the wafts of grilled seafood, citrus and rose water
guide you to Zenon Taverna. Co-owners Dora and Stelios Papageorgiou dish
up cuisine from Cyprus, and after 24 years, Stelios can still be found greeting
customers with a warm smile, sharing joyful tapestry-like stories, as if
they are guests at his daughter's wedding. While Dora runs the kitchen,
the buoyant Stelios can be found making his daily 5am outings to the local
fish market, where vendors always set aside the freshest fish for "Junior".
The crispy, succulent, chargrilled octopus is worth adding on to the
16 gorgeous dishes that already make up the notable Kypriaki Mezedes
platter, including *tarama* (red caviar) and *ortikia* (quail eggs). The bottom
of the menu reads "siga-siga," meaning "slowly-slowly". No rushing the
smorgasbord here.

# NYC AFTER DARK:
## clandestine cocktail bars

*Masterful mixology*

Here in New York, seasoned barkeeps present cocktail menus as long as novellas and readers pine for sequels. Camaraderie keeps the industry uninhibited and the so-called "bartender crush" means the pros enthusiastically swap recipes and concepts over mixed drinks (or a, ahem, beer), keeping each other creatively motivated. Good for them, and for us.

Milk & Honey may be long gone, but with today's fixation on the craft drink niche the list of specialty bars here has grown exponentially. Leading the pack is **Noorman's Kil** in Williamsburg, which carries over 400 whiskeys ranging in origin from Scotland to Japan to India, and pours up a potent tasting flight. The 19th-century bar accented with wooden cabinetry will surely take you back to old Americana. For Brooklyn-based mixology, few places beat the inviting back patio space at **Maison Première** in Bedford-Stuyvesant, where a sanctuary of secluded seating is surrounded by foliage and the warm glow of lights.

If you're a Chartreuse connoisseur, then **Pouring Ribbons** on Avenue B in Manhattan is for you – it stocks vintage liquors dating back to the 1940s. Meanwhile, those with bittersweet palates can enjoy over 50 amari and digestifs at the handsome tile bar inside **Amor y Amargo**.

The 48-hour party people in the Lower East Side can keep their cans of Pabst to head-crush later, but for those two-hour party people who seek Zen, there's **Bar Goto**. Owner Kenta Goto, a Pegu Club veteran, emphasizes the philosophy of omotenashi, the covert hospitality of anticipating guests' needs. Meticulously thought-out libations

Meanwhile, those with bittersweet palates can enjoy over 150 amari and digestifs at the handsome tile bar inside **Amor y Amargo**.

The 48-hour party people in the LES can keep their cans of Pabst, but for those two-hour party people who seek Zen, there's **Bar Goto**. Owner Kenta Goto emphasizes omotenashi, the covert hospitality of anticipating guests' needs. Meticulously thought-out libations are executed with sublime refinement, as seen in the sakura martini, made with sake, gin and maraschino liqueur, and garnished with a salted cherry blossom.

**Attaboy** is located amidst dive bars, but the push of a discrete bell opens the door to rousing tipples and handwritten tabs at this saloon that harkens back to the Prohibition Era. Former Milk & Honey barkeeps Sam Ross and Michael McIlroy prescribe the tastiest bespoke drinks with a chemist's precision.

Located inside Pier A Harbor House, **BlackTail** imagines what a bar in Cuba might have felt like in the 1920s. Its beautiful ceiling fans and framed black-and-white photos by Vern Evans make for perfect conversation pieces while sipping on sour daiquiris. It's almost too easy to order all four flavors – lime, banana, pineapple and strawberry – and drink them all dry.

Looking for a showstopping spot in Queens? Two words: **Dutch Kills**.

ATTABOY

### AMOR Y AMARGO
443 East 6th Street (near Avenue A; Alphabet City)
+1 212 614 6818, amoryamargony.com, open daily

### ATTABOY
134 Eldridge Street (near Delancey Street;
Lower East Side), +1 855 877 9900, nowebsite
open daily

### BAR GOTO
245 Eldridge Street (near East Houston Street;
Lower East Side), +1 212 475 4411, bargoto.com
closed Monday

### BLACKTAIL
2nd Floor, Pier A Harbor House, 22 Battery Place
(near Battery Place; Battery Park), +1 212 785 0153
blacktailnyc.com, open daily

### DIRTY PRECIOUS
317 3rd Avenue (near 1st Street; Gowanus)
+1 646 685 4481, dirtyprecious.com, open daily

### DUTCH KILLS
27-24 Jackson Avenue (near Thomson Avenue;
Long Island City), +1 718 383 2724, dutchkillsbar.com
open daily

### MAISON PREMIERE
298 Bedford Avenue (near South 1st Street;
Bedford-Stuyvesant), +1 347 335 0446
maisonpremiere.com, open daily

### NOORMAN'S KIL
609 Grand Street (near Leonard Street; Williamsburg)
+1 347 384 2526, noormanskil.com, open daily

### POURING RIBBONS
2nd Floor, 225 Avenue B (near East 14th Street;
Stuyvesant Town), +1 917 656 6788
pouringribbons.com, open daily

# NYC AFTER DARK
## nocturnal supper spots

*Late-night nibbles*

New York has many hidden gems for those still on the prowl long after everyone else has called it a night. At 1am, service staff from Michelin-starred establishments zombie-walk toward Manhattan's Koreatown for post-shift imbibes and dishes at **Miss Korea BBQ**. For a post-theater snack, **Casellula** dedicates an entire page (with small font) to a wide array of cheeses; this is where contrasting texture, sweetness, and tang all come to meet.

In the West Village? Head to yakitori specialist **Takashi**, where an all-beef broth ramen is served after-hours on Fridays and Saturdays – but note that you'll need a reservation.

Celebrity chef sightings often take place in the wee morning hours at **Great NY Noodletown** in Chinatown, where aromatic bowls of wonton noodle soup are the name of the game. The late-night chef at Chinatown's 'round the clock establishment **Wo Hop** prepares perfectly steamed fish and succulent snails that boggle even sober minds. There's only one kitchen here, but the staff refer to the downstairs seating as "Americanized" whereas upstairs, the authenticity is found on the whole head of a flounder. Take heed.

At sunrise, in-the-know cab drivers jump-start 4am shifts with lentils and samosas at 24-hour **Punjabi Grocery & Deli** in Alphabet City. For the traditionalists, head to **Scarr's Pizza** in the LES for a classic slice, personal pie or fresh garlic rolls.

Owner and pie slinger Scarr, a veteran of Lombardi's, makes pies with quality ingredients from dough made of stone-ground flour to sauce made from scratch using fresh tomatoes. Bonus: the back dining room blasts old-school hip-hop and resembles a high school friend's basement.

During the wee hours in Brooklyn, go for the taco salad at **El Cortez**, a tiki bar and Tex-Mex oasis in Bushwick. In Williamsburg? The booths at 24-hour taqueria **Grand Morelos**, usually fill up at 3am as late-night revelers tuck in to satisfying Milanese tortas, tacos al pastor and even American diner classics like a good ol' burger and fries.

## ARCHIE'S BAR & PIZZA
128 Central Avenue (at Starr Street; Bushwick)
+1 347 915 2244, open daily

## CASELLULA
401 West 52nd Street (near 9th Avenue; Hell's
Kitchen), +1 212 247 8137, casellula.com, open daily

## GRAND MORELOS
727 Grand Street (near Graham Avenue;
East Williamsburg), +1 718 218 9441
grandmorelos.com open daily

## GREAT NY NOODLETOWN
28 Bowery Street (at Bayard Street; Bowery)
+1 212 349 0923, greatnynoodletown.com, open daily

## NEW WONJO
23 West 32nd Street (near 5th Avenue; Koreatown)
+1 212 695 5815, newwonjo.com, open daily

## PUNJABI GROCERY & DELI
114 East 1st Street (near Avenue A; Alphabet City)
+1 212 533 3356, facebook.com/PunjabiGroceryDeli
open daily

## SCARR'S PIZZA
22 Orchard Street (near Canal Street;
Lower East Side), +1 212 334 3481
scarrspizza.com, open daily

## TAKASHI
456 Hudson Street (near Barrow Street; Greenwich
Village), +1 212 414 2929, takashinyc.com, open daily

## WO HOP
17 Mott Street (near Mosco Street; Chinatown)
+1 212 962 8617, wohopnyc.com, open daily

# jackson heights and corona

## elmhurst, forest hills, murray hill

---

Queens contains a wonderful mishmash of Southeast Asian, Latino and Indian cultures and cuisines. The infamous 7 Train runs parallel through Roosevelt Boulevard, the main artery, where you'll find fresh Thai food, multiple ceviche stands and a lady who flips arepas until 5am. The 7 Train's penultimate stop is in Flushing: handy for tennis buffs in town for the U.S. Open and where Chinese dumplings reign. The residential hum of lawnmowers and exotic aromas from crispy panipuri emanate throughout Jackson Heights. Koreatown on Northern Boulevard and 149th Place, in Murray Hill, is filled with karaoke bars, barbecue restaurants, refreshing naengmyeon and dirt-cheap soju. The densely populated storefront signs (sans English), along with the aroma of spices, are telltale signs of authentic culinary fare – and it's all just a 30-minute commute from Grand Central Station.

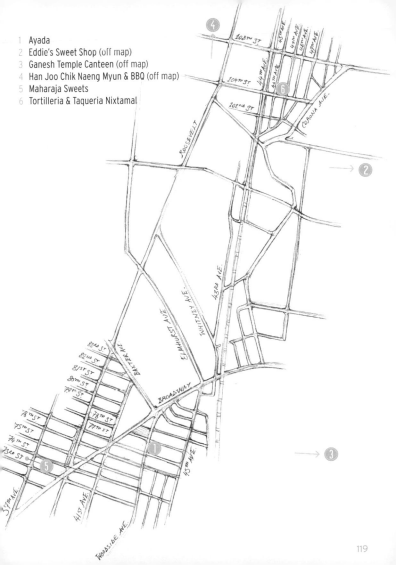

1 Ayada
2 Eddie's Sweet Shop (off map)
3 Ganesh Temple Canteen (off map)
4 Han Joo Chik Naeng Myun & BBQ (off map)
5 Maharaja Sweets
6 Tortilleria & Taqueria Nixtamal

# AYADA

*Homestyle Thai*

**77-08 Woodside Avenue (near 77th Street) / +1 718 424 0844**
**facebook.com/AyadaThai / Open daily**

An old schoolmate of mine, who'd left her family in Thailand to open a restaurant, once explained how to rate a Thai restaurant based on its spicy star indicator system. Through her tutelage I'd find myself inherently skeptical when four stars denied a sweat mustache, and no star became a just cause to break open a bottle of Pepto. Ayada sits quietly on a residential street, and chef Duangjai Thammasat specializes in northeastern Thai cuisine. Using only fresh chilies, Ayada's two stars will make you want to order a glass of beer – or two – so you can grin and very happily bear the delicious spiciness.

# EDDIE'S SWEET SHOP

*Turn-of-the-century ice cream parlor*

**105-29 Metropolitan Avenue (at 72nd Road)** / **+1 718 520 8514**
No website / Closed Monday

I almost had a major meltdown when I tasted Eddie's Sweet Shop's ice cream. Overdramatic? Not even close. Just one sip from a cream soda induced a flashback to tasting malted chocolate for the very first time. Vito Citrano has run the shop since the late 1960s, improving past recipes and making everything from flavored syrups to butterscotch sauce by hand. Having had only four owners since the turn of the 20th century, Eddie's Sweet Shop's original hardware remains untouched, from the leather-bound stools to the 1920s icebox freezers. Whether it's an orange cream or a banana split, such vivid euphoria of saccharine bliss just might trigger creamery catharsis.

# GANESH TEMPLE CANTEEN

*Dosa sanctuary inside a Hindu temple*

**143-09 Holly Avenue (near Browne Street)** / **+1 718 460 8493**
nyganeshtemplecanteen.com / Open daily

I can't quite say this place is hidden due to the exemplary use of signage dispersed throughout The Hindu Temple Society of North America: cursory signs with red arrows point down multiple flights of stairs, which means you can't miss the entrance to the cafeteria-style counter. Here, 20 different varieties of paper-thin, smooth and shiny dosas, various uttappam (thick dosas) and tiffin-style appetizers are made fresh daily. Everything is very orderly with receipt numbers booming over a mic system, and specialty food is prepared fresh. Don't let the overwhelming menu throw you off: the numerous weekend specials, cone-shaped ghee roast, and vada (snacks) with their accompanying warm vegetable chutney and cooling coconut, ginger and chili sauce are hard to beat.

# HAN JOO CHIK NAENG MYUN & BBQ

*Samgyeopsal barbecue specialist*

**41-06 149th Place (near 41st Avenue) / +1 718 359 6888**
**No website / Closed daily**

For 360 days of the year, my fastidious mother cooked strictly Korean meals. The remaining few meals were eaten out at Korean restaurants. Leaving my mother's venerable prep table to rest allowed me a chance to order delectable obscurities: "Let's order something mom wouldn't make…" sounds less insulting in Korean. The trade-off often involved listening to my mother's critique of how dinner was heavily salted. Once I started choosing my meals more independently, it wasn't until a visit to Han Joo Chik Naeng Myun & BBQ, while eating crispy pork belly, when I recalled the same discerning tastes and standards from childhood. The seasonal specialties, such as *naengmyeon* with springtime turnip-greens kimchi, or the standard classics will surely not disappoint the adventurous eater, nor the industrious Korean mother.

# MAHARAJA SWEETS

*Homemade Indian treats and desserts*

**7310 37th Avenue (near 73rd Street)** / **+1 718 505 2680**
maharajacatering.com / **Open daily**

Aside from their delicious chaat, Maharaja Sweets is best known for
the comprehensive assortment of authentic Punjabi and Bangladeshi
desserts sold by the pound. The restaurant and shop is tucked away within
the sweet spot of Jackson Heights (or Little India). Barfi studded with
pistachios or perfumed with rose water melts at the touch of the tongue.
The ras malai is fresh, creamy and has developed a cult following. There's
usually a line out the door for their beautiful gift boxes filled with colorful
sugary treats, but trust me, these morsels prove good things do come to
those who wait.

# TORTILLERIA & TAQUERIA NIXTAMAL

*Masa tortillas made from scratch*

**104-05 47th Avenue (at 104th Street) / +1 718 699 2434**
**tortillerianixtamal.com / Open daily**

Stepping into Tortilleria Nixtamal's underground prep kitchen, it's hard to believe that such a tiny space stores, soaks, cooks and grinds whole kernels of hominy and churns out 1,600 pounds of creamy masa every day. Owner Shauna Page says the tortilla machine, manufactured in and flown over from Mexico, produces 30,000 organic, kosher disks daily, which are delivered to more than 50 local businesses. For the restaurant, only local meat, seafood, cheese and naturally rendered lard are used, and while New York lunches are notoriously hasty, here the pace is as indulgent as their creamy tamales. So I certainly have no qualms in ordering another round of tacos as I wait for my tortillas to be weighed and packed up.

PIER 17

EAST RIVER FERRY

# stunning skyline views

*Bright lights, big city*

I'm a sucker for views. Whether on a commuter ride on the **East River Ferry**, or peering out from the Whitney Museum terrace, or, quite honestly, within the 10-foot floor-to-ceiling windows in the bathroom stalls of **The Boom Boom Room** at the Standard Hotel, which offer an astoundingly fantastic panorama, reminding one of the vast magnitude, energy, excitement and glittering nostalgia of NYC.

**Pier 44 Waterfront Garden** is off the beaten path deep in Brooklyn's Red Hook, and offers a fantastic view of Lady Liberty. It's located past an open parking lot and off a desolate marina dock, and you can choose to rest on one of many benches that dot the pier to take it all in.

Another quiet spot with an immaculate view of the Manhattan skyline is **WNYC Transmitter Park**, which formerly housed radio transmission towers in Greenpoint. In 2012 it was turned into an impressive green space, including a large open lawn that's perfect for picnics.

A born-and-raised resident of Queens once begged me not to reveal **Anable Basin Sailing Bar & Grill**, a Long Island City secret where mainly locals enjoy a beer and a hot dog along a boardwalk deck. Thanks to this native New Yorker maven, the adventurous can walk past what looks like a sanitation subsidiary and sketchy industrial warehouses to the very end of 44th Drive for a truly magnificent view of the sparkling lights of Midtown.

It's not widely advertised, but the Metropolitan Museum of Art is donation based, meaning the open-air rooftop view from the **Met Roof Garden Café and Martini Bar** can be enjoyed whether you pay the suggested donation or use rummaged change. Overlooking Central Park, it's a rare vantage point (unless you're visiting a friend's condo along Central Park West) that puts you in the middle of the abundant foliage and reveals a beautiful amber ombre during the autumn.

### ANABLE BASIN SAILING BAR & GRILL
4-40 44th Drive (near Vernon Boulevard; Long Island City), +1 646 207 1333, anablebasin.com, open daily

### EAST RIVER FERRY
East 35th Street and FDR Drive (Midtown East) +1 800 533 3779, eastriverferry.com, open daily

### MET ROOF GARDEN CAFÉ AND MARTINI BAR
1000 5th Avenue (near East 82nd Street; Upper East Side), +1 212 535 7710, metmuseum.org, open daily

### PIER 44 WATERFRONT GARDEN
Pier 44, 290 Conover Street (near Reed Street; Red Hook), +1 718 677 0258, publicgardendesign.com/pier-44-waterfront-garden-red-hook.html, open daily

### THE BOOM BOOM ROOM
The Standard, 848 Washington Street (at West 13th Street; Chelsea), +1 212 645 4646, standardhotels.com open daily

### WNYC TRANSMITTER PARK
West Street (at Kent Street; Greenpoint) +1 212 639 9675, nycgovparks.org, open daily

WNYC TRANSMITTER PARK